THE WHOLE WORLD IS BORN NAKED

Justin Ashford

NAKED EYE BOOKS

PURE PEACE

BORN
NAKED

ISBN:1519499574
ISBN-13: 978-1519499578

DEDICATION

This book is dedicated to my late grandmother Elsie Dorothy Chattoe, my father Peter Anthony Harris Ashford, my mother Yvonne Margaret Ashford, my brother Nicholas Ashford and my brother Adam Ashford.

ACKNOWLEDGEMENTS

Thank you to all my family and friends, you know who you are. Thank you to Sam Wall for working with me and transforming my cover design into an excellent piece of illustration (samwall.com). A very special thank you to Dr K. Gallacher for all your support and patience.

CONTENTS

FOREWORD

This book is written in diary form, the idea behind this was to see if I could write a poem every day in five minutes for the duration of 2013. My different moods reflect in the poems and they are all quite different. I hope there is something in the book that every person can relate to. A lot of things changed in my life prior to 2013 and things seemed to slot into place and words and ideas were flowing in abundance through my mind.

Justin Ashford

JANUARY 2013

January 2013
1 Tuesday

PEN TO A WHITE EMPTY PAGE

January, obsolete
Nothing personal
Better left out
Like Mondays
Boring, nothing to shout about
What difference is a Monday to a Friday?
Or January to December
Stamped in our minds
Set in stone
We would rather go straight to the good times.

2013 January
Wednesday 2

NO WINTER SO COLD

Feelings
Emotions
Good times
Pleasure tokens
New and old
No winter so cold

January 2013
3 Thursday

THE PAST AND THE PAGE

The new year is upon us
The past no more
Comfort in a new beginning
I'm not so sure
A page is turned over
The other page left behind
The old year gone
Was it intriguing?
I'm sure you will find
Upsets and deaths
New life and fun
Let's see where it takes us
Hopefully, no hardship done
The page was empty
Now it's been filled
No more crying
Over milk that's been spilled
The past and the page!

2013 January
Friday 4

A LINE WITH A STITCH

A stitch can repair and mend
Coats, trousers or a face
Sewing in a straight line
Silk, cotton or lace
Changing clothes
A confidence that's there
Old clothes, still good enough to repair
So don't throw them out
Mend with a stitch
From the old jacket to the new
Change, make the switch
When the face is hurt by a cut
Thank goodness for the needle and thread
We wouldn't want a nasty scar
On our body, face or head
Plastic surgery, why?
For surgeons to fix
Grow old gracefully
We know it's a bitch
But the beauty's inside you
No need for a line with a stitch.

January 2013
5 Saturday

I WANT HER

Next week I'm going to be
The man I want to be
Today I am that tragic man
Tomorrow is for change
A future with her I wanted
Today I'm going to arrange.

6 Sunday

HER SONG

No one can upstage her
She is number one
Taken from the Gods
Release her into song
She's perfect enough
To sing about
Madonna, an icon
Beautiful and strong.

2013 January
Monday 7

SUBSIDENCE

A piece of wood
Saw something good
Build a house
Something substantial
For our family and mouse, Mickey
Our home is of solid foundation
Full of that word, elation
A dwelling where we reside
Let's hope the house doesn't subside.

January 2013
8 Tuesday

A WISH IS GRANTED

I've become very small
Small enough to fit into a bottle
Encased into darkness
I don't eat
Occasionally sleep
On my own
Not following sheep
No change of clothes
A distinctive smell to the nose
It's very boring
Where I have been stored in
The good thing is
I make dreams come true
Make a wish, 1,2,3
So here I am
A genie, that's me!

2013 January
Wednesday 9

I DON'T LIKE BULLIES

I saw a passer by
She started to cry
I asked if she was ok
But before she could say
A man behind her started to hit her
So I stepped in to calm things down
She said to me, "don't worry, this man's my boyfriend"
"He's acting like a clown"
I said "leave her alone"
He said "it's nothing to do with you"
"Turn around and go home or I will hit you too"
So I felt sorry for this man
Because his fears are inside
One other thing I have to say is
"Bullies, I cannot abide"

January 2013
10 Thursday

W.F.T.M

Psychiatrists, Psychologist
Sociology, Societies
Chemistry, Biology
Psychodynamic, Humanistic
Methodology, Musicology
Neurological, Biological
Association, Transcendentalism
Solution, Evolution
Structuralism, Functionalism
Extrovert, Introvert
Superego, Alter ego
Association, Disassociation
Personality, Reality
Today, Tomorrow
Joy, Sorrow

2013 January
Friday 11

THE DRINKER

I used to be an avid drinker
Now I am back to the old poet and thinker
The pub used to call and find me
My excessive drinking days are behind me
I suppose I had to get it out of my system
But sometimes, those days, I still miss them
I used to love the days of having the crack
But now they have taken a seat at the back
Occasionally they spring up for a laugh
But inside, people don't know the half
I still go for the odd pint or two
There's one in my hand right now
So cheers and here's to you!!!

January 2013
12 Saturday

APOLOGISE

Sorry to leave
Sorry to grieve
Saying sorry is a relief
Sorry once
Sorry twice
Sorry for being so bloody nice
Why say sorry?
If you don't mean to
Anyway, this sorry is meant
And this sorry is for you
Sorry!

13 Sunday

LOVE IN FULL FLIGHT

If the heart had wings
Could it fly?
It would fly towards your direction
Bring a tear to your eye
A heart that flies
Beats so fast
Love in full flight should always last

2013 January
Monday 14

THIS BABY IS DEAD

Waking in a sweat
What lies beneath
Trying to forget
A raging machine
Dark dreams
Feels unclean
Like a drug
But no drugs used
A horrible portrait of a picture
Left feeling confused
Now not asleep
A patch of doubt
At the top of the heap
Sweep the dream away
Radical feelings
Swabbing the deck
One's mind floor
Is the dream real?
This baby is dead

January 2013
15 Tuesday

AT ODDS WITH NATURE

Passing the tree
Growing's the sound
Flowers are free
So is the ground
Walk and listen
With freedom
Nature's colours
Earthly tones
Peaceful at will
Being alone
Just nature's noise
No city distraction
Pure honest satisfaction
Breathing fine air
A slight exercise of the body
There's a man over there
Watching birds
Bloody hell
It's Bill Oddie.

2013 January
Wednesday 16

MONEY/CHANGE

Beggars on the street
Every step or two
Charity workers
Stopping folks in their tracks
People are strapped for cash
Can't afford their mortgage
Rent or government tax
Beggars' belief
Hard up streets
Money towards
A good cause
These days, it's your own cause
That needs charity
Maybe the country
Will change for the better
Everybody's waiting
For that day to arrive
People will still make money
But will they be fortunate?
To strive in life.

January 2013
17 Thursday

I DON'T KNOW WHAT TO WRITE

I don't know what to write
It gives you a fright
When you don't know what to write
Write a loving message
That would be nice
Not a nasty letter
Just out of spite
I don't know what to write
Do you think It's because I'm not that bright?
No, I just don't know what to write
How about in my imagination?
That might bring something to light
Like James Brown
My problem seems way out of sight
I don't know what to write
I have got to think of more in-depth thoughts tonight
Ah, I know what to write
Turn over to the next page.

2013 January
Friday 18

MAKE A GENUINE CLAIM

Time to recompense
Time to spend a penny
Insurance companies out there
Make lots of money off many
So if you have an accident
Don't be afraid to make a claim
After all these years gone by
My pain, still remains the same
If one is hurt
Make a genuine claim.

January 2013
19 Saturday

CHINESE WHISPERS

A tale that one tells
Could cause some trouble
Chinese whispers
Can make trouble double

20 Sunday

NEVER ENDS

A round circle
Never ends
A continuous line
Going round and round
Never ends
If a circle were human
It would have no friends
Continually moving
Never ends
It doesn't stop for anyone
Never ends

2013 January
Monday 21

A HOT BEVERAGE

Making a morning drink to start the day
Making coffee at work
Making tea
Which do you prefer?
It's tea for me
Caffeine in coffee
Caffeine in tea
Puts the spring in your step
Gives you a boost of energy
Coffee and tea
A drink most of us drink
Does it keep the brain working?
Or does it slow you down?
Making us tired
I am going to shut up now
And let you get on with your work
As you might get fired
Anyway, I am in the coffee shop
Drinking a cup of tea
Which I have just acquired.

January 2013
22 Tuesday

A PILLOW POEM

A pillow used to rest your head
Lay down your noggin on the bed
The pillow's soft, comfortable and cool
I don't use two pillows as a rule
Pillow talk, I don't do that
You could let the cat out of the bag
A pillow used for a peaceful sleep
Some people drown in their pillow
When they cry and weep
A pillow fight can be fun
But I would rather get my head down
Until the morning sun.

2013 January
Wednesday 23

AN UNTIDY LAKE

A bicycle thrown in the lake
Who threw the bike in there?
They need a good shake
Messing up our environment
Spoiling our view
Who wants to see a rusty old bike in a lake?
I don't, do you?

January 2013
24 Thursday

P. LARKIN

The North Ship came sailing in
Larkin, was he dark within?
Think for a second
The librarian's mind
Ladders to high windows
Time to put aside
Jazz is in the air
From blue tones to books
This poet is rare
A certain gravitas
Words up in the air
A stern but graceful stare
P. Larkin, a truth on the page.

TAKE A CHANCE

A man once said
Take your time
Find out what's on the inside?
A void of nothingness
Or a void with light
A void with a heart
That beats at night
Night time falls
Daytime calls
The next day of life is a blessing
Lucky to have that chance
A new day to have faith and dance
Take everything you can
Strive for life
Take a chance.

January 2013
26 Saturday

LIFE IN NUMBERS

1, 2, 3
Who do I want to be?
3, 4, 5
Great to be alive
6, 7, 8
Where is the white gate?
9, 10, 11
Is there a heaven?
12, 13, 14
Inside the voices scream
1, 2, 3
Who do you want to be?

27 Sunday

SUNDAY'S PINT

Sunday for a drink
The best time for a pint, I think
Relax and have a short
Maybe a single or a double one
Then go home
Put the dinner on.

2013 January
Monday 28

BROKEN DAYS

Broken days
Torn in two
Half a day
See the whole day through
Rest, wake, move
Days like glass
Smashed to bits
Until daybreak
A hammer that hits
Broken days we will fix
Smashing days thrown into the mix
Put the days into a cast
Let them heal
Smashing days
Not broken
Seem to appeal.

January 2013
29 Tuesday

BE BOLD, DON'T FOLD

Watch and be watched
Look and be looked upon
See, then be seen
Hide and disappear
Be re-born
Not torn into a life of despair
Repair your troubles
Halve them, don't make them double
Take life by the hand
Heads are not meant to be buried in the sand
When you think you are down the river and sold
Try and be bold, don't fold.

2013 January
Wednesday 30

THE SMELL OF WAR

Take the hill
Flag on top
Soldiers of fortune
Can they stop?
Drop the bomb
Push the button
Nuclear war
Napalm storm
So damn raw
Break the bank
Fight the bad fight
Air raid shelter
Strike a light
Over the decades
War has destroyed
Families and countries
People's tenacity
Stronger than you think
When crushed down
Taken to the brink
The smell round war
There has always been
That disgusting stink!!!!

January 2013
31 Thursday

THE SOCIAL CHAMELEON

The social chameleon
Makes his change
Social re-arranging
Always changing
Fickle by chance
Taking everyone on
At their own game
Adapting in a social situation
With imagination
Known to be seen
Changing behind many screens
Social gatherings
Blends in with everyone and everything
If you look deep into the soul
You might see one
The social chameleon.

FEBRUARY 2013

February 2013
1 Friday

SUICIDE, A CONTRADICTION

The first thing I said
Was the first thing I said
To not withhold of Squalor
Forward with haste to the end of days
Thou shall not move or follow
Tiny steps, move in mind
Regrets are few and far between
So if one does not make it along the way
The end of days, will never been seen

2013 February
Saturday 2

MOVEMENT OF FEELINGS

Put one's heart to the test
Let it fall down
Not in jest
Look love in the eye
And eyes will look back
Immense feelings shudder
Like electricity on a train track

Sunday 3

FREEDOM

Nature's way is to work and rest
Naturally conforming to society
Play is in there, somewhat amiss
Me, I would rather fly and be free
An individual, that's me!

February 2013
4 Monday

WEYMOUTH 1976

Golden sands burn the soles of the feet
Children happily playing
Grandparents sitting in their deckchair seats
The waves, listen, what are they saying?
The heat is powerful as if we are in Spain
But we are in England's pleasant land
Castles and trenches made out of sand
People's faces, happy aglow
The sun is scorching here in Weymouth
You won't see the snow
Ice cream sellers, candy floss and tea
Their little huts facing the sea
A walk down the beach, a Punch and Judy show
The donkeys' bells swaying to and fro
All in the dingy, ready to row
In the bar at night, songs, cards and magic tricks
Wish you were here in Weymouth 1976.

2013 February
Tuesday 5

FALSENESS

Less is more
More or less
She is filled with tenderness
Golden locks, curled at the right spot
Touching the nape of the neck
Pretty face, her smile beams
Is this woman what she seems?

February 2013
6 Wednesday

CEMETERY

An eye for an eye
Teeth for teeth
Past the gates
Home for the dead
Bodies lay beneath
Headstones, flowers
And written names
Never forgotten in mind
Young ones, old ones
The grace of the good
The mystery of the not so kind
Black is the colour
Clear are the tears
Peaceful, not a sound
Except for the whistling birds in the sky
That fly around the town
Long black cars
Drive in with the boxes
Some ready to burn
Bodies lowered to be buried
The living waiting for their turn.

2013 February
Thursday 7

X144

When the leaves on the tree fall up
We know there is something wrong
If they fall to the sky
Instead of dropping to the ground
We know the world is upside down
If we climbed a tree and fell out
Would we fall to Heaven?
Or would we fall to the floor?
Either way, who or what would break our fall?
The pavement or God?

February 2013
8 Friday

A DAY MISSED

A day missed
Like a day in the mist
Nothing moving
Nothing seen
Only a mean dream
You don't want to see
Brain is attacked
Like spears thrown at the head
I have misspelt the word daed
I mean dead!!!!!

2013 February
Saturday 9

BRAIN TRAIN

Days sometimes the same
Crushed with thoughts
Of superior intelligence
They get a bit mundane
Train the brain to refrain
From the insane thoughts
How to keep them at bay
Ronnie Kray.

Sunday 10

SUNDAY TENTH

Weak and woll
I mean rock and roll
Takes its toll
Words get re-arranged
I am not deranged
Just making things change
Hopefully for the better
It's usually worse.

February 2013
11 Monday

IT IS WHAT IT IS

The book, the look
It took, not too long
This shook me up
Like the rook
On the chess board
Pressing on forward
Hopefully not back
Or sideways
Then the hook
Gave me the buzz for writing
And this was not mistaken
For being just a faze
One was amazed
And the words
Are still cooking in my book

2013 February
Tuesday 12

4 X 4

Four by Four
What's the score for?
Am I flawed?
Or am I flawless?
Turn the corner
Handled like a dream
Then the crash
Then the scream
Broken bones?
No, broken soul
Deflated air bag
I feel let down
Turn a corner again
Will I come around?
4 x 4, I wouldn't drive one at all
But I keep driving through life
Overcoming all of the hurdles
Until the final call.

February 2013
13 Wednesday

GREY HAIRED MAN

The man walks
The route of time
Same dress, same address
Does he find what is out there?
Or is he masked?
Hiding from the decay
Walk this way, every day
Reggie Kray

2013 February
Thursday 14

I HAVE RUN OUT OF THOUGHTS

I have run out of thoughts
Will I outrun the ticking clock?
Battered inside and out
Will I be escorted to the grave?
Like tiny particles
Settling on the ground
Nothing but dust
Will I be blown away?
Like an electric fan
Cooling the sweat from the brow
Is this all there is now?
Nothing left.

February 2013
15 Friday

TOO MANY EUR'S

Flower power
Eisenhower
Blackpool tower
Man power
Girl power
Percy Thrower
Electric shower
Shut that dower- slang
Higher or lower
Sweet and sour
Self-raising flour
Try and wow her
Grass mower
Leaf blower
Boat rower
Take it slower
Rock and roller.

2013 February
Saturday 16

FEELING PRETTY DAMN SHIT

Past the doorway
Down the stairs
Broken sleep
Tired bones
Into the kitchen
Leave me alone
Ahh, a nice cup of tea.

Sunday 17

POTATO PEEL SUNDAY

Peel the outer skin
The potato inside
Put the peel in the bin
Meat and veg, gravy on the side.

February 2013
18 Monday

THROW US ME BOOTS

Throw us me boots
Feel uprooted
Suited and booted
Shout to the top
"Throw us me boots"
Put them on
Out the house
To the pub, on route.

2013 February
Tuesday 19

If I WERE A CHAIR

If I were a chair
All day long
I would sit there
In a room with a view
Take a pew
Comfortable and sturdy
Relax, listen to Donavon
Hurdy Gurdy man
Like the chair
On its own
Most of the time, all alone
Then someone would sit down
The chair has no choice
Would it scream if it had a voice?
I would rather be a chair to be admired
And looked at, rather than being used
But some big fat bottom is there to abuse
If I were a chair, would I be leather?
If I were a chair, would I be cloth?
Or flea bitten, by the material eating moth.

February 2013
20 Wednesday

MOMENTS CHANGE LIVES

Moments are used
In so many ways
Do you act upon them?
If one does not make use
Will you get that chance again?
A moment in time
Maybe a split second to react
To lay down your tracks
A special moment
A bad moment
A quiet peaceful moment
Magic moments
The romance of a moment
Moments change lives.

2013 February
Thursday 21

T.L.O.A.D

The line of a diary
What's it for?
To write down the next line
Like before
Making words come into play
Bursting out of the page
About memories every day
Again, past, present and future

February 2013
22 Friday

10 YEARS TODAY

EDC, a lady who is very special to me
Ten years gone by
Missed every day
Within my heart
Yesterday, today and always
She, a woman who was kinder than kind
Instilled within her daughter
Still remains
Angels spring to mind
White feathers are left for us to see
To make sure we feel peace and tranquillity
So, who is this person?
Heaven is where she lies
Ten years gone by
This lady is my nan
The tears run dry.

2013 February
Saturday 23

DISCO

A few drinks
Down the Gregory Peck
Chilled out, sat down
DJ starts playing at the discotheque
1978 on a plate.

Sunday 24

HEY DICKHEAD

Down by the church
Near the Old Grand
Folded fists, clenched tight
Both hands ready for the fight
Splattered by a cup
Grief again, following me around
Like a cancer, fighting its way through society
Why can't they leave me be?

February 2013
25 Monday

DOES THE SUN WEAR SUNGLASSES?

Does the sun wear sunglasses?
Maybe, maybe not
The sun's reflection would be too bright
Perhaps the sun would rather be the moon
And come out at night
Which glasses would the sun choose?
Wayfarers or a classic Ray-Ban
Does the sun leave it to the moon to wear the glasses?
The moon is too cool
Wear them, she can!

2013 February
Tuesday 26

PETANQUE IN THE SUN

Derelict, ruined, a quiet ruin
Sun blazes down across the Med
Rippled ocean, see life in the old town
Old men playing petanque, not a chore
Smiles on their faces, as the jack leaves their hands
And rolls along the dusty clay floor.

February 2013
27 Wednesday

I'VE BEEN LOOKING FOR YOU

Happy being, drive on at will
The prediction will be made by the profit
The inevitable day will come
Not just for me, for you and then some
They will look for you and find
Prophecy through the mind
Meet your maker
Not the destruction taker
This day will come true
I've been looking for you.

TOP CAT

Top Cat, he is the boss
Waistcoat and hat
He's some cool cat
Fancy, Brains and Benny the ball
Always scheming to make that score
Watch out, here comes Dibble
He knows Top Cat's on the fiddle
Top Cat with his dollar bill on a wire
Give up the sharking game
Top Cat will never retire
Sleeps in his bin
Ear plugs and mask
He is Hip hop
Top Cat!!!!!!

MARCH 2013

2013 March
Friday 1

MONDAY WAS LAST IN THE QUEUE FOR BEING LIKED

What did Monday do wrong?
Bleak weather gives Monday a bad name
Most people would remain in bed all day
The colour blue is linked with this day
The day before Tuesday
If asked, most people would wipe Monday off the calendar
They would probably sell this day or even give it away
Some people would skip through the week, straight to Friday
So on a Sunday, don't feel blue and get psyched
Monday was last in the queue for being liked.

March 2013
2 Saturday

T.K.O

Smell fear
Tell
Sell
Yell
Hell
Well
Ring that fucking bell
I'm throwing in the towel

3 Sunday

ANOTHER DAY GOES BY

Another day goes by
Just like the one before
Routine is upon us
Making the day become a bore
Time is pressing on
It will not stand still
If we shot the clock
We would have more time to kill.

2013 March
Monday 4

ANOTHER YEAR GOES BY

Another year goes by
Quick as the ball on the roulette wheel
Are these the cards we have been dealt?
Is this how we want to feel?
A roll of a dice, will make a choice
Year by year, swallowing our own voice
Shout out loud
Be heard, every day
Make your mark along the way!!!

March 2013
5 Tuesday

THE DEVIL INSIDE THE WITCH

CENSORED

2013 March
Wednesday 6

MAKE IT MAGICAL

Not tragic
Make it magical
Like a magician
Presenting his show
Saw the woman in half
From the stomach to the big toe
Fantasy, sometimes the best place
To get away from it all
Make life magical
Let yourself fall, fall and fall
Into the dream.

March 2013
7 Thursday

IT DRAWS YOU IN LIKE A PENCIL

HP sauce, no, HB draws
An outline delves deep into the unknown
Draws you into despair then disrepair
A run down dishevelled state of being
Turns the mind into a piece of Art
In all its glory, worth seeing
Is there life in art or an Art to life?
Construct your stencil
It draws you in like a pencil.

2013 March
Friday 8

8/8

Eight on the eighth
Henry the Eighth
808 State
One continuous line
Like a race track
After seven
No, After Eight mint
I 8 all of those
Eight times eight
64, I suppose
Four plus four equals eight
That's about eight summed up on a plate
Harry Tate!

March 2013
9 Saturday

SO AND SOW

Sow the seed
Mend the cloth
Sow the seed of love
So let the chrysalis become the moth

10 Sunday

M.J.M.N 30.40.50

Marc, John, Michael
Tree, Gun, Pills
Nearly 30, 40, 50
Should be alive still.

2013 March
Monday 11

MUSICA

Classical, Folk, Blues, Jazz
Rock and Roll, Soul, POP, Indie
Musica, so powerful
It can hit your inner soul
Like a sledgehammer to the ears
Radio, vinyl, CD, MP3
Can take you on a journey
To the Heavens
Like a bird, fly and be free
Emotions erupt like a volcano inside
Musica can make you feel happy, melancholy
Even make you cry
Instruments played, a story is told
A voice from the heart
The poet's got soul
Eggs are scrambled
That's the beat
Turn up the heat
Like a fish caught on the hook
A tramp with a riff
A stamp touched by a tongue
That's the lick
Musica, Latin for music.

March 2013
12 Tuesday

BITTER, UNTWIST IT

Bitter and twisted
Untwist the bitterness
Leaves a bitter taste in the mouth
Don't let the mouth go south
Smile, let the lips go north
Show the teeth
Dig up the happiness from beneath
Relax, untwist it, don't be bitter
Flitter away unhappiness
Saturated with morose thoughts
Can make one twisted
Untwist it, before it goes sour.

2013 March
Wednesday 13

CHILDREN WILL COME OUT OF THE WOMB AS ADULTS NEXT!

Children, wonders of our world
Let them grow as a child with a happy face
At the right time and natural pace
Plenty of time to take on adulthood
Wear children's clothing
Play with toys like a juvenile should
Keep children as children
Until the right time for them to become an adult
Teach them, look after them
Love them, be part of their lives
It should be written in text
Otherwise children will come out of the womb
adults next.

March 2013
14 Thursday

SICK AND TIRED OF BEING SICK AND TIRED

Get up, walk around
Heads on fire, feeling the burn
Joints have a life of their own
Crunching, sore, informing me constantly
Performance is down, cannot breathe
Sometimes wish I could leave
Where is the relief?
Ringing in the ears
Passing are the years
Like a crushed piece of paper
Ready to be thrown away
Deprived sleep, restless days
Bad genes, passed on
Which I have acquired
Sick and tired of being sick and tired.

2013 March
Friday 15

SYCAMORE TREE DANDY

Talent in droves
Sacred like oil from the olive groves
Electric Warrior, take one's skill
Brigid like, towards the tree over the hill
Feather boas, so he could show us
Style and grace
Cross legged with guitar, glittered face
Like the swan on the lake
Excellence and purity
Make no mistake
The warlock of love
Climb the tree of life
For a clearer view of Jesus
Look through the maple leaves and be free
Sycamore tree Dandy.

March 2013
16 Saturday

LAMPLIGHT

Lamplight so bright
On a table
On the floor
Read a book
What's in store?
Shining on the story
Waiting to unfold
In my imagination
Low and behold
Lamplight, switch off now
The story's been told.

17 Sunday

MOTHERS

Mothers, love them
They love you
With all of their hearts
An arrow right through
Mothers, what would we do without them?
Shine or rain, they are there for you
Again, again and again
Or if not, they should be.

HITLER

Hitler, barbaric
Like a coarse stone waiting to be thrown
Evil to the core
Sent from the Devil to even the score
The slick down hair
The black moustache
Raised arm, do not salute him
He didn't succeed
Taken down by the British
Help from the Yanks
I'm not writing about this man anymore
I will cut this poem short
Put down the mighty pen
The word is abort.

March 2013
19 Tuesday

DOORBELL CHIME

Knock the door
Rap the letter box
Ring the doorbell
Lift the flap
Just shout and yell
Is anybody in?
Maybe not
Maybe they forgot
To renew the batteries this time
In the doorbell chime.

I PRAY

I pray for me
I pray for you
I pray for children in need
I pray for sun, I pray for rain
I pray, so the farmer can sow his seed
I pray for peace in our world
I pray for change
I pray for growth
I pray, maybe my prayer is out of range
I pray for soldiers at war to come home safe
I pray for love, not hate
I pray for our world to be a better place
I pray for every creed, colour and race
I pray to God
I pray hoping there is a God
I pray once more
I pray, hoping that all of this will be worth living for
I pray that when we die, there is another life!!!

March 2013
21 Thursday

PAPER PLANE

As young as a child
From those adolescent days
Simple things pleased the mind
From a square white page
A paper plane was made
Formed and designed
From one's own hand
Perfectly creased
So it could be thrown, and land
Some would nosedive
A two second crash
Others glide, chasing the wind
Folded, with wings
Simple and free
Like that paper plane
I got stuck in the tree.

2013 March
Friday 22

WATCH THAT DOCK MUCK OVER THERE

Watch that dog muck over there
The dog's just left it
The animal doesn't care
The dog is not at fault
The dog cannot pick it up
So here comes the owner
Plastic gloves and bag
This sloppy owner has left it on view
Now I have trodden in it
There's shit on my shoe!

March 2013
23 Saturday

SCRIBBLED OUT WITH A PEN

Words are covered with a blackened cloud
A so called mistake
If I had used a pencil
I could have rubbed it out and started again
Sometimes humans get things wrong, now and then
This wrong is scribbled out with a pen
W---g.

24 Sunday

SUNDAY, IS IT A RUN DAY?

Sunday, is it a run day?
For some it is
Not for me
I'm a walker you see
Fresh air, a stroll with the foot
Casually gliding along
Inside, nothing's wrong
Ah, peace!

2013 March
Monday 25

WASHYO WILLY

Washyo Willy was a fine soldier
A very fine soldier indeed
Scottish to the core
With his chopper
He would lead
He would stand to attention
At the drop of a hat
Salute to all the women in need
Washyo would rumble in the jungle
Make his way through the bush
Pouncing without having to rush
Washyo Willy, clean as a whistle
Prickly and determined
Like the emblem, a thistle
Willy, will he rise
Perform like a Trojan
Come into the night
Washyo, bring the unborn into the light.

March 2013
26 Tuesday

A TACTICAL CALCULATED MASTER

Calculations are there
Tactical thoughts
Ideas from the brain
One should not procrastinate
Be the master, use words wisely
Entirely for the grace of the good
Hoping great wealth of life will come, touch wood
Confidence, coincidence
Luck, cause a stir
Make people think
Change your way from the dredge and the stink
Use the power of the mind
Let your thoughts get a speeding ticket for driving faster
A tactical, calculated master.

2013 March
Wednesday 27

IT'S A PLEASURE TO SAY YES

Saying yes should mean
You want to do what has to be done, when asked
It's a pleasure to say yes
An empty pause gives the rest of the page
Time to think of something else, more or less
It's a pleasure to say yes
Giving one's love and time
Helping others rest
It's a pleasure to say yes.

March 2013
28 Thursday

A JOKER AMONGST MOST

Are fools fooled?
Is eating fowl a foul
Take a fork, eat a joke
Laugh out loud until you choke
A joker amongst most has had his day
Look to the real host
Thirteen for dinner
Food and wine
Make the toast
Wash the feet of the people you meet
With humility
Him or her
The Last Supper.

2013 March
Friday 29

PRE-RESURRECTION BODY

A tortured walk
A carried cross
A thorn blooded crown
Crowds looking on the sentencing of death
Brought upon this town
Crucifixion, a sacrifice
A pure spirit and soul
Our Saviour will be born again
To forfend he or she
Pre-Resurrection body.

March 2013
30 Saturday

SATURDAY, SATURDAY, SATURDAY

Saturday, Saturday, Saturday
What's the matter with you?
I say
Fed up, bored
Going for a pint if I may.

31 Sunday

AN EGG

An egg is hatched
Born for the first time
A resurrection rhyme
Chocolate, hardboiled
Born, an egg.

APRIL 2013

April 2013
1 Monday

THE FOOL ON THE BRIDGE

The fool on the bridge
Glances around
There's no one there
Just his lonely stare
Dormant feelings have rushed up to the surface
Nobody's perfect
Looking over at the cold, grey Thames below
How deep?
Is it shallow?
Wallowing in his own tormented struggle called life
What is he trying to end or begin?
What's with him?
Is this his solution?
Committing sacrilege
Who is the fool on the bridge?

2013 April
Tuesday 2

SIBLINGS TERRITORY

Laying down their own mark
Tempers are frail
Take a deep breath
Calm down, inhale
Making silly remarks
Insults a trade
From one to another
So called brothers
All has gone for a moment
Will it be found again or remain sour?
Who has the power?
One sided, one thinks
Mouth is sewn tight
No need for the fight
No glory, Jackanory
Siblings territory
It happens all the time
End of story.

April 2013
3 Wednesday

GUNS

Guns, silver and black
Crimes associated with them
Usually money, war or crack
A gun does not kill unless picked up by the hand
Ending somebody's life
I don't understand
Maybe I've misunderstood
Guns are good
I don't think so
Will they be banned?
If not, they should
A pistol, rifle, a sawn off shotgun
Killed by a piece of metal
No more sun
Used in wars, past and present
I suppose in the future
It seems to be the way
Say no to guns
Have your say
Stop the killing.

THE SOUL OF A SOLDIER

Has a soldier got soul?
It's waiting to unfold
Mapped out, waiting to be told
What would a day cost?
If it were to be sold
How old are days?
A day is one
The soul of a soldier
Is it still living?
Has it left and gone.

April 2013
5 Friday

CYNICAL CLINICAL

Pessimistic, distrusting
A clinical cynic
Rewind, erase
To start new days
Change the future
To change the past
Begin again
Let it all pass
Leave the mind clinic
You jumped up cynic
Have you reached your pinnacle?
Cynical, Clinical.

2013 April
Saturday 6

GYPSUM TEDDY

A master plasterer
Gypsum Teddy's the man
His walls are as smooth as silk
Like condensed milk from a can
His work as a plasterer
Keeps him afloat
They wouldn't lace his moccasins
Gypsum Teddy
He need not gloat.

Sunday 7

RICH FIX, POOR FIX

Rich fix, poor fix
A great divide
Twists and turns
A rollercoaster ride.

April 2013
8 Monday

HUMOUROUS LOVE

Take a flower
Draw it to one's chest
The heart is a flutter
Keep one step ahead of the rest
Look at her eyes
Silky with a glint
I wonder if she would buy me a pint?
Because I'm bloody skint.

2013 April
Tuesday 9

SET YOUR ROCKETS OFF

Attraction with distraction
Fatal but loving
Person to person
Tense adrenalin
Excitement within
Bubbling to the surface
So many emotions and feelings
It's ready to leave
The other waiting to receive
Launch from the dock
Set your rockets off.

April 2013
10 Wednesday

IS THE SUN A MAN AND THE MOON A WOMAN?

The sun and the moon
How can we tell what sex they are?
Is the sun a man?
Is the moon a woman?
Work it out if you can
The sun does shine
The moon's too cool
King or Queen
Which one would rule?
No, they are not people
The moon is a satellite
The sun is a star
Many miles away
Admired from afar.

2013 April
Thursday 11

SLIDE IT TO THE BRIDGE

Twisting, turning
Out of control
Nothing shaking man
You've got no soul
Take it to the bridge
Unleash the fire
Slide it to the bridge
Down to the wire
The moves are hot
Fire and ice
Slick and cool
Smooth and nice
The dance is the action
The body is the light
Strike up the passion
Into the dark night.

April 2013
12 Friday

CORPORATE COMPANIES WEAR MASKS

Corporate greed
The seed has been sown
Into the gutter
People are thrown
Money, money, money
The big wigs
They are not
Your honey bunny
Trouser seams are strained
Their pockets are full
Taken from the downtrodden and vulnerable
Dick Turpin wore a mask
So do the corporate companies
They just take
They don't ask
Excuses from the rich
Squalor for the poor
Put down the gun
Away from the head son
Don't take it anymore
Let the poor take the gun and turn it on the rich
See how they feel, when they become our bitch.

2013 April
Saturday 13

A BREAK IN THE CIRCLE

Round and around
A continuous line
Full circle, everything's fine
A band of gold
Together as one, two souls
Keep the faith
A break in the circle
Divorce it makes.

Sunday 14

TAKE, TAKE, TAKE

Take, Take, Take
Fake with the faker
Bake with the baker
Take from the taken
Shake with the movers and shakers
Too much taking rather than giving.

April 2013
15 Monday

MONEY FALLS

When money is calling
In church, on a plate
Which bank will give us the best interest rate?
Money comes, money goes
Slips through our fingers
Right under our nose
Money favours the rich
Beats down on the poor's door
Money can eat away at your heartstrings
Right to the core
Does money grow on trees?
If not, it should for a while
So we can all have a bite of the apple
Make our face produce a smile
Money falls through our hands
Because we like to spend
It would be rude not to
One wouldn't want to offend!

2013 April
Tuesday 16

NICOTINE SID IN HEAVEN

Nicotine Sid knocked on the pearly gates
Sid said, "hurry up Peter", "I'm dying to see my dog and you're already late"
Peter let Sid in and Sid said "hello"
Peter replied "stop being cheeky or I will send you below"
"When can I see my dog?" Nicotine Sid asked
Peter said, "slow down, not too fast"
"first you have to take a test, before you can rest"
"Bloody Hell" Sid said
"It seemed like it was all a test when I was living"
Peter said, "you would still be alive with your wife,
If you were a little more forgiving".

April 2013
17 Wednesday

I JUST NEED ANOTHER TITLE FOR THE BOOK

Running out of words
Don't be absurd
Is it writer's block?
No, I'm from good stock
Cows on a farm
No cause for alarm
The words will return again
To write with a pen that's black
Just like the sheep's wool
It will always grow back
Pigs in their pen
Rolling around in the mud
The cows seem happy chewing the cud
Water still flows past the trees from the brook
Words are still flowing
I just need another title for the book.

2013 April
Thursday 18

A SHIRT COLLAR

A shirt collar
An Oxford scholar
Starched pristine white
Collars up or wear them down
Maybe a grandad would be nice
A button down
Cutaway or wingtip
Like a cowboy
They would call you Rogers
First name Roy
Trigger is his horse
Why not be formal?
With a shirt collar, and follow with a tie.

April 2013
19 Friday

A BLANK POEM

Read this one
If you can
Maybe it's there
Without knowing
A blank poem!

2013 April
Saturday 20

THE SLICK CAT IN THE TRILBY

The cool cat in the trilby
Plays his trumpet until he cannot play anymore
Cool and smooth, so raw
Tilted hat, sweat pours down the face
The light glistens off the brass
Finishes his piece until the room is still
At this moment the master craftsman is free
The cat in the slick trilby.

Sunday 21

A FISHERMAN'S COLD

The wind blew in from the harbour dock
Germs were passed, a cold and cough
This job as a ship's mate
Feeling unwell at fast rate
Cannot get warm
From head to the toes
Wish I could stop this runny nose.

April 2013
22 Monday

THE WOMAN WITH THE SILKY SKIN

The woman with the silky skin
Blonde, tall and thin
Smooth and tender
Lovely Linda
Skin like glass
Silky as silk
Perfectly white
Complexion like milk
Rose red lips like a china doll
But with real flesh
Heart and soul
A smile to match
Oh what a catch
Beauty inside
Beautiful within
The woman with the fine silky skin.

2013 April
Tuesday 23

MOANERS MOAN

Moaners moan
A snarl and a groan
Creased face
Worn lines
Crow's feet
Chicken's neck
Bloody heck
Moan at this
Moan at that
Cease the moment
It's usually flat
Grumpy old men
I'm one of those
Grumpy old men
On the street
On the bus
In the car
In the pub
In the house
On the phone
Moaners moan.

April 2013
24 Wednesday

A CAR SHOWROOM SALESMAN

A car showroom salesman
Sales they make
Pull the wool over your eyes
Make no mistake
Commission on tap
So they think
"Would you like a coffee sir?"
"No thank you, I've just had a drink"
Cars are gleaming, shiny and new
"Is the car to take the kids to school?"
"Or is it just for you?"
"I think I will go for a used car"
"Not brand new"
" Are you sure sir?"
"I can do a better deal for you?"

2013 April
Thursday 25

A BOTTLE WITHOUT THE MESSAGE

Floating, drifted to an artificial beach
Seaweed, pebbles, crabs
Footprints from people's feet
A washed up bottle
The corner of the label remains
A clear glass with a tint of cobalt blue
A jagged edged top
The cork half bitten through
No paper message inside
Maybe washed away with the tide
Possibly, thoughts blocked from the writer's hand
Lonely like the ocean
Without it's marine life
Years at sea
A bottle without the message
Has made its way onto the sand.

April 2013
26 Friday
MY Birthday

THE WHOLE WORLD IS BORN NAKED

Stretched stomachs, tiny heartbeats
Amazement waiting to come into this world
Male or female
A wonder at that
What will the child become?
Possibilities are endless
Reproducing another human being
It's closest to a miracle, I think
Reproduction, do we need instruction?
No, closeness will happen
Love will always prevail
Every single human has at least one thing in common
The whole world is born naked
Peace, peace, peace, peace.

2013 April
Saturday 27

NOTES ON A BLANK ENVELOPE

Notes
When to vote
I wrote
On a blank envelope.

Sunday 28

A SWEET VOICE ON THE END OF THE PHONE

A soft sweet voice
Customer Services
Imagining a beautiful woman
On the other end of the line
Why am I so alone?
A sweet voice on the end of the phone.

April 2013
29 Monday

MOBILE MADNESS

Lifted to the ear
Always that fear
Of missing that call
Addictive
Vindictive messages
Mobile madness
Implies sadness
Modern technology
Cannot put it down
Constantly waiting
For movement
From the corporate fruit
Billions and billions of pounds
Extracted from the general public
Makes one feel sick
The contradiction is
I am becoming the same with mine
Stop, put it down
Use the tin string tin line.

2013 April
Tuesday 30

THE BOY WITH THE DUSTBIN, BRUSH AND SHOVEL

The boy with the dustbin, brush and shovel
Spending time doing chores
Sweeping other people's floors
Working for free
Perhaps he feels free
That's his freedom
Simple but kind
The job, not his mind
Twigs and brambles
Dirt and leaves
Who is this boy?
Where is his family?
What are his wishes?
What are his thoughts?
At peace with himself
Doing other people's chores.

MAY 2013

WHO OWNS WORDS

The owner of words is the voice and hands
The spoken word or written down
Re-arranging letters
Changing words around
We all use similar words
But in a different way
Do not plagiarise other people's written work, I say
Construct your own story or song
Plagiarism is wrong
Who owns words?
They belong to all of us
Do we buy?
Or do we let?
The letters of the alphabet.

May 2013
2 Thursday

DOES BUTTER FLY?

A butterfly
Does a fly eat butter?
With wings they move
A flap and flutter
Does butter fly?
I suppose it can
When it's thrown from the woman
At the man
As it is hurled through the air
Butter curdled everywhere
An argument churned up from the past
About the expiry date on the butter
It's thrown out at last!

THE STOOGE

Jim wriggle
Jim dance
Jim on glass
Jim no more on H and crack
Jim the idiot
Jim down on the street
Jim no shoes on his feet
Jim punk
Jim make my day
Jim let your music play the play
Jim rocks
IGGY POP.

May 2013
4 Saturday

NAIL CLIPPER BLUES

Nail clippers
On the shelf
All alone
Waiting to clip toenails
To fit the shoes
Only used, once in a while
Nail clipper blues.

5 Sunday

COMB IN THE BACK POCKET

1950's, creamed hair
Cool as the wind
Ready to wear
The slick pair of jeans
Dark shade with gold seams
Down at the jukebox café
Ready to hop it
Don't forget your comb
In the back pocket.

MUSIC AND WALKING

Music and walking
Free as an eagle
Steps taken
Bouncing along the concrete
Burning up some heat
Music and walking
Through the parks
On the street
In time with the strolling
The music is controlling
The dance is in the air
A walk back to nature
A slight wind in the face
Stepping into a faster pace
To the beat
Down on the street
Music and walking.

May 2013
7 Tuesday

NEWMAN, REDFORD, McQUEEN

Newman, Redford, McQueen
They are some acting machine
Butch, Sundance, magnificent too
The great escape from death
When it ricochets off you
Paul, Robert and Steve
Icons of the big screen
Films in abundance
Especially at Sundance
These guys had and have the X factor
Newman, Redford, McQueen
The men inside the actor.

2013 May
Wednesday 8

LAMB CHOP

From the sheep to the lamb chop
Then the drop
Down the mouth
Lovely juicy meat
Keeps us happy
On two feet
Brought up thinking
This was right
Eating an animal
Inside my mind
This is not normal
It feels wrong
Do sheep go to the supermarket,
and buy plastic wrapped human meat?
No, they do not
Lamb chop!

May 2013
9 Thursday

THE MAN WITH THE ONE EYED DUCK

The man with the one eyed duck
He was always running amuck
A farmer, his living he makes
His farm has fields and a lake
Actually, the lake is more like a pond
This farmer was clumsy
Always getting things wrong
Most of the ducks in the pond seemed happy
Except the little duck with one eye
The farmer had poked it by accident
When feeding the duck bread and rye.

2013 May
Friday 10

UNREAL

Unreal, no need for a meal
Imaginary, feeling non-existent
Much to my resistance
From another kind
Transported through mind
Illusory, like a magician's assistant in the box
Not there, far from above the clouds
Only to describe the sound
A whirling, twisted tornado
Waiting for the crescendo
Cannot go back or come down
Mystery is upon me
Like a psychological novel
Turning the crisp, cream looking page
Touched by a flower
The scent to the nose
A thorn to the rose
An angel in men's clothes.

May 2013
11 Saturday

HORSE

A horse of course
Has run its course
To the finish line
Masterful, sleek, refined
A horse's coat
Brushed to a thoroughbred shine
The race has been won
Out with the so called jet set
In the crowded enclosure
More winners to come
I bet.

12 Sunday

HUNTER

Hunter
Catch the serial killer
He's a monster
Track him down
Rifle through the clues
Stay one step ahead
So he doesn't outsmart you
It's only a film

2013 May
Monday 13

THE SLUGS HAVE COMMANDEERED THE KITCHEN

Slugs in the kitchen
Where is the race?
Quick, get the salt
Pour it on their face
A midnight feast
With slime and gunk
An army of them
Without tanks
Like small elephants without trunks
The slugs have taken over the kitchen
The battle has been won
If only I could have remembered
Where I put my slug pellet gun.

PS
No slugs were hurt in the making of this poem.

May 2013
14 Tuesday

YMA

Very kind
As you might find
Respect, as you expect
Caring and fair
Do people really care?
Loving and trusting
Tenacity is a thirst
Beauty and beautiful
Young hearted and fruitful
Angel of angels
Generous to a fault
Intelligence in droves
Modest, not like most
Family comes first
Funny and fun
Hardworking
Work, never left undone
Everyone treated equal
Peaceful and tranquil
Best of the best
How a mother should be
Very special
A spirit that is free.

2013 May
Wednesday 15

WHY DO WE?

Why do we hurt?
Why do we curse?
Why do we eat so much?
When we are fit to burst
Why do we ask?
For things all the time
Why ask this question?
What's the next line?
Why write a rhyme?
I suppose, to pass the time
Why are we here?
Ask the man
He will give you a sign
Why, why, why?
Why do we say goodbye?
God be with you

May 2013
16 Thursday

GO ON, HAVE A SING

Singing in the rain
Singing in the dark
Singing in the light
Singing at the park
Singing in the sun
Singing with the larks
Singing in the shower
Singing in the bath
Singing at the top of your voice
Sing from the heart, if that's your choice
Sing when you want
If you don't want to sing anymore
It's up to you, then don't.

2013 May
Friday 17

HOW'S YOUR HEALTH THESE DAYS?

How's your health these days?
Chronic, sprawled out, worn out
Drained like a drip through a tube
Alzheimer's, sometimes confused
Slow, like a mule
Feeling a bit foolish
Drab days, the same
Week in, year out
The armchair flower pattern
Torn and worn through
Overused, no fault of her own
Staring through the same window
Same window
Same routine of dreaded misery
Waiting for the wooden box
How are you feeling today?
I think this old lady has answered my question
In her hospital bed as she lay
Drifting away.

May 2013
18 Saturday

CHASE AFTER THE CAR THIEF

Here we go
Wearing underpants
Nothing else on
From head to toe
Chase the car thief
Up the road
Scrape the back of his collar
Can't get a hold
Off in his motor
With his assailant
Go, go, go
At least he didn't nick my car.

19 Sunday

TREACLE TART

Treacle tart
Can make you start
Feeling very windy
So when it does
Let one go
Sniff, it smells cringeworthy
So when you start
Your treacle tart
Enjoy!
Don't worry if it makes you puff and dart.

A TORN HEART, A TORN PAGE

A torn heart
A torn page
The heart ripped inside
The page in two
Something has died
Constant dread
Spoken words
The woman cheated and lied
Notes on the page
Trying to work out
The words of deceit
No shakiness from the pen
Solid words, too confident
Lies in full amount
The letter torn from top to bottom
Thrown in the bin
This woman is evil as sin.

May 2013
21 Tuesday

CLEAN EVIL WAY

Newspapers
Many words in print
Where are my glasses?
I'm beginning to squint
Stories of crime, rape and robberies
Sometimes a horrible world
Paper swept down the road
A wind and a whirl
Trash on the concrete
Trash walking the streets
Put out the rubbish
Take out the trash
Beat down the door of crime
Recycle the garbage
Let the evil do their time
Clean the streets
Clean the evil feet
Sweep it all away
Let the clean in
Let the grace of the good stay
Until the end of days.

2013 May
Wednesday 22

RECORD OR DOCK

A record token
A token gesture
A token of affection
A broken record
Acetate, a circle direction
Black, a sweet liquorish colour
A hole in the middle
Put the needle on
Scratch the surface of the vinyl
Songs belting out of a long oblong box
Record players rock
I'd rather the turntable
Than the mp3 dock.

May 2013
23 Thursday

AS I PLEASE

Talk to the avenues
The pavements are listening
Walk down the next block
Footsteps are drowned out
Like a man in wet clothes
Nobody hears, does anybody know?
Follow the rest of the ants
Newspaper in hand
Hot dog stand
Candy store land
Where do the pretty people go?
Home, to work
Waddling to and fro
I'm the tourist
I can come and go as I please
New York, a moment to seize
Fellow rocker streets
Lou Reed, Lou Reed
As I please, as I please.

2013 May
Friday 24

SHE THINK SHE'S SMART
THE MONEY COLLECTOR

Looked up to
Talked down to
Passed round like a parcel
Ready for the next child to unwrap
Falling into the trap
Dollar bills
Caught in a corrupt world of greed
I feel the need
To be stern and straight to the point
Ridiculous amounts
Building up in interest
They should ring in normal hours
Before anger kicks in
Put to the test
Calm down, let it rest
Put it to bed and rest.

May 2013
25 Saturday

TAP DANCER

Cancer
No answer
Cancer
Fight Cancer
Battle with Cancer
Back to Cancer
Tap dancer

26 Sunday

BOOKS, BOOKS

Books sold
Books bought
The information inside them
Scholars are taught
Books black
Books burnt
Reading through them
A joy to learn
Books start with the writer's hand
Paper made from trees
From our glorious land
Books, books.

I AM OF MANY FACES

I adapt in different social situations
I adapt to instruction
I adapt with confusion
I adapt with the downtrodden
I adapt with the forgotten
I adapt for my sanity
I adapt in big cities
I adapt in small villages
I adapt with the rich and poor
I adapt in the temples and churches
I adapt with the people who are trying
I adapt when nothing is left
I adapt when talking to beautiful women
I adapt to musical tastes
I adapt to the government in place
I adapt so the world is a better world
I adapt through different fazes
I am of many faces.

May 2013
28 Tuesday

LIFE IS WORTH LIVING

Sad but not sad
Love but not loved
When push comes to shove
Push can shove it
Move and be moved
Moved without moving
Approved by approaching
Approached but removed
Taste without tasting
Touched but not touching
Appearing to appeal
Appealed not appealing
Heard but not heard of
Hard of hearing
Reveal without revealing
Revealed and relieving
Alive but not living
Lived but not lived in
Forgive the right person
Because life is worth living.

2013 May
Wednesday 29

A BETTER BRITAIN

Evil blood
Turn to water
Noah, where's the flood?
Change the picture
Dictators are out
Choice is in
Without a doubt
Cut the head off sin
Fighting for something
So they think
Brainwashed Britain
Is it about to sink?
A country in decline
Used to be refined
Churchill's people
Powerful but kind
It needs to change
For better, not worse
That's why I am writing this verse
People join together
Stop the hate
Mr Cameron
Sort this out
Step up to the plate.

May 2013
30 Thursday

THEY FOUGHT WARS ON THIS STUFF

War always leaves people distraught
When needed, they drank the brown tea leaves
with water
Enough to comfort the heart
A strong cup of tea
Put's the fight and strength in Britain
Bringing solidarity in a cup
Soldiers, people of Britain
Together as one
So remember when things get really tough
Put the kettle on, drink tea
They fought wars on this stuff.

GOING ROUND IN SQUARES

To go round in circles
Drives you up the wall
Travelling on a continuous line
Going round in squares changes the course
At least you can turn from time to time
Change the shape of your destiny
Sometimes there's a more positive route
Get off the outer circle
Turn a corner
Wear the shoe on the other foot
Or maybe buy a pair of boots
Change your destiny
Even if it's slight
If you don't
You may regret it one day
Don't always turn left
Occasionally turn right.

JUNE 2013

2013 June
Saturday 1

TERRY AND JUNE

Terry and June
Terry loved June
The month he loved most of all
Happy to see the 1st of June
Because it was May no more.

Sunday 2

A LONELY DEATH

A lonely death
To God she goes
Nobody at her funeral
No worries, no woes
Sad to think
She was on her own
She didn't whine
She didn't moan
A lonely death
No flowers in her window
Curtains closed.

June 2013
3 Monday

DO DOGS WEAR BOOTS OR SHOES?

Do dogs wear boots or shoes?
Only if their paws are sore
Bulldogs in Doc Martins
A Shih Tzu in slip-ons
Alsatians in black leather goose stepping boots
A Corgi would wear a Prince's slippers
Dogs of royalty wouldn't follow suit
A Greyhound would wear Nike to run faster round the track
They would definitely catch and munch on that virtual rabbit's back
Poodles would wear high heels with a matching handbag
A Chihuahua would go bare paw
Because she would worry about the price tag.

JERRY DROPPIT AND HIS IMAGINARY ELECTRIC SHED

Jerry Droppit lived up to his name
Always dropping things
Again and again
In his imaginary electric shed
That's where he dreamed he was
In his magical head
Electric shed, electric shed
Jerry Droppit had no friends
They all dropped him
Like he dropped things
He didn't need them
He was happy on his own
In his imaginary electric shed
There Jerry could drop this and drop that
Without anyone calling him a clumsy clot
Jerry's imaginary electric shed
In his mind, it was electrifying
Peaceful, his own space
Away from the rat race
Jerry Droppit even had a clumsy looking face
Jerry Droppit and his imaginary electric shed
Do you think he could stop it?
Before he dropped it.

June 2013
5 Wednesday

NOT A FULL BAG OF CRISPS

Not a full bag of crisps
Half a bag
You look inside and you lose your rag
Not a full bag of crisps
What a rip off
The good old days
They used to be full
Nowadays you can count them on one hand
This is from one of the popular brands
Come on, fill the bags up
You have enough money
Times are tough
Let us enjoy what we pay for
A nice tasty snack
Not lack of crisps in a bag
When we see the crisp bag
Its shape should be plump
Not anorexic looking
That just gets our backs up
And gives us the hump
Not a full bag of crisps.

2013 June
Thursday 6

HERE WE MOW, HOW FAST DOES YOUR GRASS GROW?

Here we mow, here we mow, here we mow
How fast does your grass grow?
Spring and summer months
The grass is so green
Sun and rain
The grass grows very fast, so it seems
Here we mow
Here we mow
Here we mow
How fast does your grass grow?
Through the window
Looking at the garden
It has grown so fast again
Since I cut it recently
The power of the sun and rain
The lawn mower is looking worn out
Might have to buy a new one
Nothing to shout about
Here we mow, here we mow, here we mow
Here we mow, here we mow, here we mow
Here we mow, here we mow, here we mow

June 2013
7 Friday

LOWRY

Lowry from Stretford, in tune with his roots
Matchstick men painted in their hobnail boots
Cats and dogs, men and women
Drawn like thin logs
Children playing, smoking stacks
We laughed so much in Manchester
We nearly had heart attacks
Men in bowler hats
With their walking sticks
Textile mills
The colour, a shaded grey and brown mix
Lowry, honoured in Salford
The museum at Salford Quays
A man that is admired
His paintings seem to please
Charcoal drawings on napkins
Too clean to feel a sneeze
Industrial landscapes
Man lying on a wall
And a market scene
L.S Lowry, Manchester has his heart
His artwork there to be seen.

2013 June
Saturday 8

A DOOR HANDLE

An Irene Handl
A door handle
Push or pulled
Open or closed
Is somebody on the other side of the door?
There could be I suppose
Open the door and find out
Oh there is nobody there
Good, because I would rather be on my own
With peace and quiet
So I don't care.

Sunday 9

A PEACEFUL SILENCE

A peaceful silence
No sound
Except a slight noise from a bird
In the distance
A relaxing moment
Frozen sound
Giving peace
Making time for Heaven
Before it melts
A peaceful silence
Is what I felt.

June 2013
10 Monday

A PLACE YOU DO NOT WANT TO GO AND SEE!

Pole to pole
Coast to coast
To the broken and shamed
The Devil's the host
Grit fine sand
Burnt out beach
Icy cap, Heavens out of reach
Stretched to the limit
Fire and ice
Lizard skin man
There to entice
Scaled to new heights of desperation
Escorted down the escalator of damnation
It's too late, you won't get back
Having to leave what you thought was home
Now you're in the damned death zone
Best to keep on the straight and narrow
Because you've seen nothing like this before
And you wouldn't want to.

HARRY TATE

Harry Tate
Married to Kate
The Tates lived at number 8
Cressington Place
Harry looked like Charlie Drake
His favourite singer was Tom Waits
I saw him the other day
He looked a right state
Always had things handed to him on a plate
I used to work with Harry Tate
Always bloody late was Harry Tate
I saw him Saturday night
Coming home from the pub
I heard his wife Kate, shout
"Harry, where have you been?"
"Get up, put yourself straight"
As he tripped over the garden gate
He ought to slow the drinking down
He will snuff it at this rate, Harry Tate
Harry Tate, being a fool was his trait
Harry Tate, I used to hate
He wasn't my mate
Waste of space
That bloke Harry Tate.

June 2013
12 Wednesday

MOTORWAY ROAD

A motorway road
On the stone, all that metal
Congestion, a foot on the pedal
Articulated lorries, vans, cars
All going about their business
Up and past, moving straight
Keeping the mind focused
Trying to concentrate
Trying to reach where they are going
Not being late
The rain can fall on a motorway road
Making the car harder to control
The heat can beat down
Making you feel uncomfortable and stuffy
Loosen the shirt and tie
As other vehicles speed by
Turn off at the next junction
To get home to your abode
Off the motorway road.

2013 June
Thursday 13

TURNING TABLES

Turning tables
Turning chairs
Dancing around them
Like Fred Astaire
Take your woman
Don't sit down
Fling her round
Give her a spin
Make her feel special again
Dancing on the tables
Dancing on the chairs
Turning tables
Because you care
Don't let love get stale
Turning tables round
Let love inhale
Show her some moves
Show her some love
The tux and the bow tie
The scarf and the gloves
Show her you're able
To turn the tables.

June 2013
14 Friday

THE DOG AND PARTRIDGE

The dog and partridge went into town
For a couple of pints
The dog asked the partridge
"What would you like?"
The partridge replied
"A Brandy Alexander would be nice"
The partridge said to the dog
"What are you having?"
The dog replied
"A nice ice cold bottle of beer straight from the fridge"
The barman then said
"How come you two are in here?
"You are usually at your own pub, The Dog and Partridge"
The partridge said to the dog
"That bird over there is nice"
The dog replied, "damn right"
The Partridge said
"We could go to her pub after this drink"
The dog said "yes, it's called The Feathers, I think"
The dog then said, "that bird's mate is a nice little bitch"
The Partridge said "yes, after The Feathers we could go to her pub"
"The Dog and Duck"
The dog then said
"If we play our cards right tonight, we might get the f—k".

2013 June
Saturday 15

TUTTI-FRUTTI MAN

Tutti-frutti
Seller on the beach
Pineapples, bananas
Oh, what a Peach
The fruit man selling his health
Tanned women
Gorgeous and toned
Melons passed around to be eaten
Sun loungers on loan.

Sunday 16

A WOODEN SPLINTER

The wooden splinter
Has become extinct, yeah
Abstracted from my finger
Pulled out in two
Half left in
Soon taken out
Not left to linger
It was that splinter in my finger
Lodged, deep and sore
It made me cry
Do you know why?
Because I'm a little girl aged 4.

June 2013
17 Monday

LEARN TO LIVE WITH THE VOICES

Echoes inside
Ringing, constant churning
Battling with your own conversation
Like an ocean, dark, murky, vast
Drowning in the depths of one's own subconsciousness
Voices, overpowering with slow overbearing chatter
Speaking, repeating, over and over
Returning to the mind, like a mobile ringtone
Waiting to be answered
Arguing with your own self
Then losing the battle
Repent, fermenting inside
A crushed bubble bursting
Spraying all around the mind
A thousand voices sharing their thoughts at once
Scrambled egg, like mush
Tiredness kicks in like a mule
Feeling like a fool
A bloody crippling battleground
The war comes to a halt
Stop! Turn to the voices
Speak with them
Make them your friend
Accept the inevitable
Answer their questions
Pupils reply to their teachers
Why can't we?
Learn to be free
Learn to live with the voices.

GARY GRANT, SHIRT, TIE, JACKET AND PANTS

The screen is hit with his aptness of eloquence
Grace on his arm, charm and elegance
A movie star, a crisp and cool gent
Grant brings the screen alive
A character played well in Hitchcock's eyes
North by North West
Cary at his best, thrown to the ground
He comes to a stop
The plane dusting him down and shadowing the crop
Eva Marie Saint, how can he restrain from her distraction?
The beauty, the glamorous, the instant attraction
Watching the film, the audience's satisfaction
A smooth dapper man in grey
Cary Grant, shirt, tie, jacket and pants.

June 2013
19 Wednesday

LUNCH AND INSULTS

I ate a nice cold sandwich
From the Earl of Sandwich
With a glass of wine, there to sip
Hunger pangs kept at bay
I ate a nice cold sandwich
Very nice, I say, I say, I say
There is always someone there to spoil your lunch
Obscenities were a trade
I thought the insults from across the room
Should be kept at bay
When I finished my wine and sandwich
I thought I would have my say
Before I left the restaurant
I told the man eating his sandwich
To mind his bloody language!!!!

2013 June
Thursday 20

A MESS

Tidy up
Put the plates away
Wash the cups
Sweep the floor
Mop it again, once more
Hoover the stairs
Dust down the chairs
Clean the oven
Clean the bathroom
Especially the loo
Don't forget to clean one more thing
You!

June 2013
21 Friday

LIFE IS – YOU HAVE TO LIVE IT

Life is
All around
Life is
Here and now
Life is
Not forgetting, it's time to put on a show
Life is
Choice
Life is
Making your mark, let them hear your voice
Life is
Being your own person, stand out from the crowd
Let them hear you, shout it out loud
Life is
Full of surprises
Life is
Full of fun and optimism when the sun rises
Life is
Forever living from start to the end
Life is
Like an ally, life I will defend
Life is
Magical, it should be your best friend
You didn't ask to be born, now you're here give it a go
You have to live it, make it your one man/woman show.

2013 June
Saturday 22

5 WORDS

Words in music
Words in books
Words in pictures
Browse to look
A world of words
A spoken voice
Worldly wise
Words in a pop-up book
Read to children
A nice surprise.

Sunday 23

TASTE THE SUN

Taste the sun in the sky
Raise your game every day
Taste life, the sun is smiling
So then will you
So powerful, changing moods
Feeling good about the day
We all have to begin
The sun is God's smile
Like a parent
Next of kin.

June 2013
24 Monday

BURST THAT RUT BUBBLE

A thick outer circle
Like an overcoat
Made from soil and sin
Dark, textured, tortured soul
Burst that rut bubble
Put you, the maker of your destiny, back in control
Take the knife, slash and carve
Cutting it in half
The rut bubble can burst
Particles spraying, pinging, releasing the energy
Freedom on tap, like bursting bubble wrap
Burst that rut bubble
I know it's easy to get trapped
Take out the samurai sword
Cut through the bubble
Crisp, clean and neat
Get back in the game
Take on the driver's seat
When the bubble bursts and floats down to the
floor
The bubble has gone; it hurts no more
Time to move on
Take on the future
See what's in store!

THE HAT HE CHEWED

The hat he chewed
Had some attitude
Cool, grey, hat of the day
Smoking hot, Sinatra style
A beautiful woman
The fine weathered hat
Tipped once in a while
Sophisticated, like a lounge lizard as he sat
The man lost the bet
The poor chap had to keep to his wager
And eat his hat.

June 2013
26 Wednesday

I NEED TO THINK OF A MASTERPIECE

Is this piece a masterpiece?
Thoughts waiting to be born
In an embryonic state
The foetus, there to be seen
On the screen
Could this be an abortion?
A miscarriage of words
Don't be obscene
A form of peace
A child coming into the world
My baby is born
Revealed onto the page
A boy or girl
A miracle nurtured from start to the end
A contrived birth shows its worth
The power of words was not rehearsed
In ore of this poem
My baby is growing
Life on the page
Now at toddler stage
One page to a full book
The child is, but not living
The poem is alive
Words, letters, sentences
In life they will arrive
I need to think of a masterpiece
Have I brought this one up well?
A child, a person, the poem
This is the end; can you tell?

CAKES AND WEIGHT

Flavours, textures
Cake bowl mixtures
In the mix
A wooden spoon
Have you got room?
For some more cake
Chocolate, sponge or a cream doughnut
Lots more cakes to bake
But don't eat too many
You will put on weight
For heaven's sake.

June 2013
28 Friday

RE-ARRANGE YOUR HEART

Re-arrange your heart
To coincide with mine
Day by day, I still love her
I will make her mine in time
She loves me but she keeps away
Too proud to make that change
Don't be afraid to re-arrange your heart
Live life with love in mind
Make that start
Pull on the heartstrings of love
Pull on the hair of love
Let it play, let it grow
Love will overflow in everyone
If you re-arrange your heart.

2013 June
Saturday 29

TREMOR OF THE HAND

Tremor of the hand is slight
Is there something sinister going on?
Or is it the alcohol I consumed last night?
Too much overindulgence
Abusing the body's temple
Should I lead by example?
But then again would I get bored?

Sunday 30

THE BATH OVERFLOWS

Water rising
She falls asleep
The bath is about to overflow
The level is reached
Water through the ceiling
Wet kitchen floor
Trickling down the walls
Like a waterfall
Wait for the argument
Ready to blow
The bath overflows
Trouble grows.

JULY 2013

INSIDE THE BRAIN OF A MOBILE PHONE

Silicon Valley
Village of the ram
Computer City
Technology implodes
What about the brain of a mobile phone?
Cellular network, radio link on tap
Printed circuit board
A keypad to adapt
The microchip subscriber identity module
Removed from one to another
An antenna, a speaker so you can say
Microphone, battery liquid crystal display
The digital signal processor
Microprocessor, that's some brain
Future technology advancement
Connecting people worldwide
That's their game
Our gain.

July 2013
2 Tuesday

SLIDING DOWN A WATER SLIDE

Sliding down a water slide in the Florida sun
Me and my sisters, dad and my mum
I wish you were here
Wish you could have come
The longest water slide in the world
Oh, what a thrill
Slipping, sliding, going faster
Water up the nose
As we reached the end of the slide
We nearly lost our clothes
We tried to see who could go the fastest
Much to our surprise
I think it was dad
I couldn't be sure
I had water in my eyes
I thought I would slide down headfirst
Instead of on my back
Guess what happened next?
Ouch, I have broken my arm
What a painful crack.

EATING A CHOCOLATE SPIDER

I ate what I thought was a chocolate spider
Usually I can confide in her
It seemed a bit crunchy to me
It's supposed to be a chocolate novelty
But when I bit down on its body
The shivers and quivers ran through me
The juices started to flow
A real spider popped up to say hello
This did make one feel sick
It was nothing but a mindless dirty trick
The woman I thought I could trust
Was always picking a fight
So the spider I ate that night
Was real, not chocolate to bite.

July 2013
4 Thursday

A BOX WITH SEVEN CORNERS

A box with seven corners
Where is corner number eight?
Cutting corners
Mistakes will be made
If the corner of the box is cut
The right angle has gone
With the corner missing
We are not the full box, so it seems
We can rebuild it
Bring in the cardboard prosthetics team
A hole in the corner, look right in
Delve deep inside, what will we find?
Stumbling deep into the insights of the mind
A box with an angle astray, can be a strain
Turning one into a state
A box with seven corners
The resurrection of corner number eight.

TOUGH OLD GRANNY

Old granny
She was funny
Always spending other people's money
A shark at cards
A hustler to boot
She would leave her teeth out
To show us the roots
She would outsmart anyone
People thought she was thick
Clever, intelligent, sturdy as a brick
She would always dress in black
People thought she was a witch
As I said earlier, a shark at cards
Four aces, you know she made the switch
But try and prove it
You will get cut down
Old granny, strongest woman in town
The head of the clan, don't mess with her
Always sitting in her Mafioso chair
Don't look at her too long
You will get the evil stare
Be afraid, be very, very afraid
The old house maid
Tough old granny.

July 2013
6 Saturday
VIEW FROM A G STRING

A piece of string
Doesn't cover the ring
A tiny amount of thread
So sexy, enough said
Stuck up there all day long
Must be uncomfortable
Doesn't seem right
The cotton's in the dark
Switch on the light
A landscape of hills
The bottom line
View from a G string
Is it a song or words written in rhyme?
The G string has been eaten
The bottom has been out to dine.

7 Sunday
THE COLOUR BLACK

A darkened shade
Henry Ford
Black was his trade
The new black
It's the fashion
A black seat belt
Which we fasten
Black has its own hole
No other colour has a hole
Black's powerful enough
To take on the role
Black's cool, black's rock and roll.

MEAT HOOKER ON A T BONE

Hooker on the street
Tattered, torn, worn, high
Cooked, burnt out
Like a piece of meat
Chargrilled heart
Charcoaled soul
Nothing left to give
Just people there to take
Her heart is wrenched
Like a monkey twisting the nuts
On the wheels of life
Pimps are a trade
Money is made
Feelings of worthlessness
Unhappiness, no tenderness
Dredged up, dragged down
Thrown from pillar to post
Again, the Devil's pimp is the host
Picked up by men to ease their urges and desires
She wants out of the Fawkes fire
No family, no friends
Just the dregs to keep her company
On her own
Meat hooker on a T bone.

July 2013
9 Tuesday

HAND TO THE SILVER SPOON

Passed on
Money on tap
Like water through a hose
Mother and father
Love is like a drought
Left with another
A substitute mother
No time for quality guidance
Love but not loved
From the heart to a dove
More like a dodo
Extinct from nature
Dealt with a silver spoon
Swept away, like dirt and dust, with a broom
Hand to the silver spoon
Parents, too busy
No time for their children
Trying to buy their kids with money
$50, here you are sonny
Feed them, love them
Don't nourish them with money
Parents, it's time to make room
Hand to the silver spoon.

2013 July
Wednesday 10

SUP UP YOUR PINT

Sup your pint up
Time to go home
Landlord shouting
Voice like a baritone
Then the barmaid starts to shout
Drink your drinks up
Come on, get out
Doorman's angry
Losing his cool
Twenty minutes drinking time
What a stupid rule
If the staff would just leave you alone
Everyone would get up and go
Sup your pint up
You're drinking too slow
I will have to take that drink off you
If you don't hurry up
Ok, but I paid for this pint to sup
Take it from me
Don't even think about it
Because I am going to knock my pint back
And finish it off.

July 2013
11 Thursday

A CONVERSATION TO NOWHERE

That's the way
That's the road
No it's not
Are you sure?
Or have you forgot?
The competition has started
Who has won?
A mindless conversation to nowhere
Doesn't sound like fun
Has he got the better of his wife?
In full control
What's his prize?
A rollover to nothing
Evil in his eyes
Are they on the same road?
The argument, like their life together
A conversation to nowhere
Pick up your prize
You have won Ten Grand
Will the prize be shared?
Who really cares.

2013 July
Friday 12

A TRICKLING TRICKLE

A trickling trickle of water
Is but a tickle on the face
A trickling trickle of vinegar
From the pickle
Tickles the roof of the mouth
A trickle of heartfelt emotions
Can start the trickle of a tear
Down onto the cheek
A trickling trickle of raindrops
Can disturb one's view through a window
So if you get into a pickle with a trickling trickle
With a tear
A tickle on the face
Buy a tissue with a nickel
And wipe away that trickling trickle.

July 2013
13 Saturday

ARE BEES CLEVER?

Are "B" s clever or is it just the "A" s?
Hang on a minute
I am going off in a tangent
Drifting off, slightly fazed
Bees are clever
All that honey they make
Don't let them become extinct
They should have shares and a stake in this world
Honey made from bees
A beehive's their home
Orange and sticky
Honey can get you in a mess
So the answer to my question
Are Bees clever?
Then, yes.

14 Sunday

A ONE MAN SHOW

A one-man show
A lonely drifter with a cause
Class in abundance
Style, grace, generosity
Tenacious to the end
A benefactor has been sent
The lonely road ahead
Doesn't deter this true gent
Like the seed that's sown
Tolerance will grow
This definitely is a one-man show.

A CHILD TO A MOTH

A moth lands in the hand
Temptation is there
Could turn into a silken smudge
Unless tolerance prevails
A child to a moth
Most would follow the adult
Smashing, death to dust
If the adult does, the child must
As the child grows
Wings are flown
Is there a conscience?
Frustration, tolerating the insect's way
Let the moth fly free
Conquer this and one can fly free with them
Like people, let the moth breathe
Achievement will be first in the race
A better human condition
Is it such an impossible mission?
Wiping out war, racism, pure hatred
Sin, killing, fighting over religion
A child to a moth
Become the adult
Not the slayer.

July 2013
16 Tuesday

MANZAREK'S WAY

Open the Doors, the key is played
A mystical mind wrenching genius sound
He plays as if life should be fine tuned
Harmony passing by, remaining in the room
Through the Doors, watching
Sitting perfectly still and free
Echoing the lizard's voice
The Vox Continental combo organ
Played like a tempestuous ocean
Floating through the storm
Breaking through the other Doors
Four in one mind
A psychedelic find
Blues in the nite city
On the Sunset Strip
A light that is Ray
Manzarek's way
R.I.P Ray.

INSIDE MY ORIGINAL HOUSE

It's dark in here
Warm as toast
Inside my original house
Kicking, thumping
To let them know
Boy or Girl
It's time to grow
My house has got one door
Waters broke, pelvic floor
Breathe and push
So I can go outside
To see what all the fuss is about
Here and worldwide
Nine months I lived in this house
I got quite attached
Like a field to a mouse
I wonder what my new house will
OH! nearly there, one last push!!!!

July 2013
18 Thursday

REBEL WITH A CAUSE

The rebel has already landed
A cause worth fighting for
Whether it transpires or not
Push it along to the truth
Sometimes feeling transparent
Shout it out loud
Raise the roof
Knock the tiles and lath clean off
Voice one's opinion to fight evil
Crushing evilness down
Like a sledgehammer to a brick wall
The Devil's dust shall fall into the hands of the
master builder
Everybody will be alive again
In Heaven and on Earth
A shiny new floor
Rebel with a cause.

A WORLD NAMED AFTER LOVE

Time for sadness
Time for humour
Time to grieve
Thou shall not leave
Time for fun
Time to pass out happiness to everyone
A world named after love
Those days are temporarily gone
But soon will return
When we all learn to love.

July 2013
20 Saturday

SCRATCH CARD FEVER

A queue at the shops
Scratch card in hand
Paid for, supply and demand
Leave the shop with hope
Scratch the card
Sometimes, no win
Other times, money in hand
Smile on the face
Are you a believer?
A queue with scratch card fever.

21 Sunday

SUNDAY WEARS A COAT

Sunday wraps its coat around you
Keeping cold at bay
The day that is rest
Not work, Sunday best
The English way
Sunday's coat
Big enough for the whole world over
Sunday's overcoat
Protection for the working week ahead.

2013 July
Monday 22

The Fifth Wall

Inside, drowned out
Staring at four walls
Fear creeping in
Terror treads inside the head
Lost in an array of grey
Bricks, bars, no fix
Nightmare city is now my town
No smile, permanent frown
A lost child in an adult's body
Raises its ugly head
Isolation, institutionalised
Paying for the crime
Doing the time
One did not commit
A far and beyond failed spirit
Lost in the torment
Pain becomes me
Freedom, no longer free
Staring at the four walls
Day in, years repeating
Over and over
Insomnia kicks in
A mental state, can't take no more
I am nobody, I have become
The Fifth wall.

July 2013
23 Tuesday

COLD HEARTED LIAR

Croak by the tree
Stoke the fire
A permanent sinner
A cold hearted liar
Travels from place to place
A drifter, grifter
Stern, quiet face
She takes your heart
Steals your cash
Rips out your throat
The next town
She's there to gloat
About her misadventures
She needs to be on a lead
Held back from everyone she meets
Flash car, trash, lives on trashy streets
Hotels, the neon signs of grief
Taken down, like a mule to the fire
A permanent sinner
She's a cold hearted liar.

2013 July
Wednesday 24

THE CAVE IS NOT THE SOLUTION

Treachery, deceit
Recognition on the street
A full blown blow society
Crack den tramps
Trademark stamps
Pushers, stealers
Freeloading freewheelers
The needle slides in
Then soothes out
Another, then tenfold
An addicted option
Once started
Who can stop them?
Smoky lines
Cocaine face
Heroin, the place where the L lives
Inside, drastic change
A destroying ride
Destruction City is their home
Free to roam
In the dark lowlife shadows
Of frequented horror
Tripped up, tripped out
Lowlife louts
Scratched surface skin
Veins on fire, age wears thin
Constant sin, follow him, will you?
Into temptation, no retribution
A stormy treacherous road
A fall into shame
The cave is not the solution.

July 2013
25 Thursday

MAKE US A BREW

Make us a brew
In the morning
Wake me up a bit
I'm still yawning
Tea is strained
So am I
Which way does the crow fly?
Tea at breakfast
Tea at teatime
Feeling refreshed
Tea for the sake of it
Tea to pass the time
Make us a brew
While you're there
Make yourself one too!

2013 July
Friday 26

BIGOT CITY ACTIVIST

Sitting on a curb
Minding one's business
Girls of youth
Bigot city activist
Interference, across the tired looking street
Worn out eyes
Bunion feet
Clicking knees
Clicking wrist
Bigot city activist
Bigot in black should take a step back
Thinks he can control
A doorman's his role
What a bigot, a nasty soul
Anger kicks in, starting the chant
Bigot city activist
Starting to rant
Power to his head
He thinks he's arrived
Their freedom should not be deprived.

July 2013
27 Saturday

LONDON CALLED

Where I live
Had enough
London called
Off the cuff
Fantastic time
Had by all
It didn't stop
London called
No worries, no cares
While we were there
I lost my voice
Having a ball
There's always next year
When London will call.

28 Sunday

THE RECORD FOR GETTING A KNOCKDOWN PRICE

The price is high
Knock them down
Folded notes
The boys are in town
Rock and roll clowns
Debit card blues
Counting ones and twos
A toy town room
Bring down the hammer
Going once, going twice
The record for getting a knock down price.

2013 July
Monday 29

MONDAY'S SHOES

Monday's shoes
Walking towards
The Monday Blues
Take them off
Relax, don't threat
Taking its toll
Don't get upset
Monday soon goes
Tuesday's shoes are next
Follow the diary
It's written in text
Change the shoes
You've got nothing to lose
Don't let it kick in
The Monday Blues
What's with a name?
Monday, Tuesday, Wednesday
It's basically the same
Just another day
A state of mind
Remaining discombobulated
Just think it's Friday
In Monday's shoes.

July 2013
30 Tuesday

A CITY TO SETTLE IN IS HARD TO FIND

Remaining on holiday
In my old town
Looking around
Only a slight frown
Taking one's time
To relax and unwind
From just having
Another time of my life
Have a bet and a pint
Read the news
Tackle the crossword
The word is refuse
To hang around
Reminiscing
London's the town
I won't be too long
On my town's ground
Back to London
To turn things around
Having what I thought
Could be my home
London, Paris, New York
Could it be Rome?
It's time for a change in my mind
A city to settle in is hard to find.

2013 July
Wednesday 31

EXHAUSTING THOUGHTS

Try to fly
Thrive to try
By the by
Wave goodbye
See the future
Turn a blind eye
Mask the future
Visions are blind
Don't take a blind bit of notice
Sight is blackened
High is being a far cry from low
Slowdown, the lowdown is not making sense of it at all
Words rushing round
A mixed bunch juggled around
Transforming into an excruciating sound
A mishmash, a dash of thought
Slashing the thinking in half
A rush and a crush of spoken voice
Turning into mush
Leaving people mentally exhausted.

AUGUST 2013

2013 August
Thursday 1

LITTLE BOY BEN

Little Boy Ben sat on his pen
While writing a nice little song
He noticed he had misspelt
The words with his felt
The song he had written was too long
So this caused frustration
Spelling mistakes, he would make them
He thought he would shorten his notes
Describing each word on the page
Without getting pen rage
His pen was half bitten
The song was nearly written
When finished
He hoped everyone would listen.

August 2013
2 Friday

FRIDAY IS MY DAY

My day is Friday
Is it a tell the truth day?
Or is it a lie day?
Friday is the truth
Freya's day
The Goddess of love
To feel free and belong to loved ones
Loved in a free state
Not to be trapped so you begin to hate
Friday is looked forward to
From work to a slice of freedom
To take on a piece of the weekend
Slices of freedom question the rest of the week
Days, are they weak?
Or just another day?
Are days the same but with a different name?
Like us humans, similar but with our own identity
Friday is my day.

2013 August
Saturday 3

HALF AND HALF
WHAT'S THE RATIO?

To be fair
Do I care?
It's very rare
If they care
Some people do
Some people don't
If I keep staring at this poem
It might send me to rack and ruin
A message written down
For the grace of the good
Might give me the answer
If it doesn't, maybe it could
My thinking and my stare
I think this person does really care.

Sunday 4

A CUT OFF POINT

A stranger at the pub
A cut off point
A sharp stop
Release the tension
Fit to drop
Enough is enough
Can't take no more
I wish he would shut up
The bumbling bore
Jackie Phelps, tolerance should help

August 2013
5 Monday

A RUSTY OLD PUMP

A rusty old pump has had its day
Found on the common
A dull shade of grey
Laces are gone
Canvas is torn
Somebody's left it
Spoiling the lawn
To fit the left foot
What's happened to the right?
Probably in the river
Another poor sight
There was life in the old pump
Maybe sports played or just goings on
Business or trade
In fact, they look like Green Flash
Dunlop is where they're made
No, more like Taiwan
A new pair of pumps for a tramp
If he could find the other one
Well he would already have them on wouldn't he!!!!

2013 August
Tuesday 6

TANGENT CITY

Off in all directions
Voices attacking at all angles
Cannot get a word in
Tangent City
A movement of the face, a slight grin
Peace and quiet has been thrown out of the window
Tangent City, the conversation still in full flow
It's becoming a grind
All about them, selfish, unkind
Can't they take a breath?
Leave the words behind
Getting one's back up
I'm in that city
Tangent, not pretty
Not my idea of a good night out
Talked at, not talked with
I'm leaving with haste forthwith
Leaving for another city
Leaving Tangent City behind
Peace and quiet
Follow the next city sign.

August 2013
7 Wednesday

WICKED FIRE

Flames rise up
Properties burn down
Arson town
Smoke filled rooms
High rise flats
An atrocity, an atrocious act
Bodies burned, wicked fire
The match was lit
The petrol poured and tossed around
An evil arsonist playing with fire
Taking people's lives
Temperatures getting higher
Can't get out, trapped inside
The damage caused
Whoever did this should go down for life
A pyrotechnic eccentric
Places his curse on this town
Wicked fire, no more
Stop the burning down
You flame fire clown.

2013 August
Thursday 8

THE T IN TIME

The T in time
At the start
Not like the E
Further down the line
T's and E's
I's and M's
Put them back together again
You get time
Capital T for time
An important job, the letter T has got
At the start of time
Time is precious
The beginning of time
It's our lifeline
The letter T should be proud
On the clock face
Round and round
Time passes on for all of us
Time comes for the next generation
Without the T in time
We would have nothing
No time at all.

August 2013
9 Friday

NO LONGER WITH US

As cool as a rose
Hot as the fire
A downturn into a slip of a stream
She's angelic like, as she walks along
A river's edge, mellow and serine
Her feet tenderly stroke the blade of the grass
Green strands between her toes
She floats like a sailboat
Gliding, trimming through the water
Hair like the sail, fully swept back
A quickening soothing wind
Flowers are picked by her dainty thin fingers
Innocent but with an angel's wisdom
She is free, no one can touch her
Transforming into a feeling of weightlessness
Invisible, no one can see her
A silhouette curved beauty
Tender lips, auburn hair
Perfect hands and feet
The angel is no longer with us.

2013 August
Saturday 10

A SILENT GLASS

A silent glass
Not a murmur from the water
A quiet taste, an acquired taste
This poem has to be scrapped
Like a celebrity's photo
That's been taken by the paps
Don't cry over spilt water
Now a silent glass
This work needs a master class.

Sunday 11

ONE ALONE

Alone before
Alone now
A lonely figure
All alone
A loner
A lone spirit
A spirit that is free
To just be
Or to see the world
Around, away and at home
One alone.

August 2013
12 Monday

LIVE YOUR LIFE

Taken, twisted, fake them
Eggs beaten, bacon
Risks made, take them
Love, hearts, broken
Comfort, home, lived in
Story, poem, begin again
Pride, passion, jealousy, refrain from
Fashion, clothes, wear them
Music, soul, instrument
John Winston Lennon
Sky Blue Heaven
Hell, sin, learn your lesson
Shout, fight, stop aggression
Money, banks, institution
Repent, penance, Retribution
Nobody, everybody, somebody
Imprisonment, remain out of trouble and strife
Live your life.

2013 August
Tuesday 13

MY CAPITAL A

A bouncing ball
A bird's mating call
A result that raises a smile
A feeling you haven't had for a while
A day full of surprises
A day without crime would be nice
A meal at the Chinese, number 23 with egg fried rice
A year without grief and sacrifice
A troubled author that's hit a brick wall
A new pen that will trigger off the gun of writing
A world full of people, surrounded by peace, no fighting
A letter that is the start of everything
A letter to start the day
A letter that is A capital A.

August 2013
14 Wednesday

DO YOU WANT HALF A PORK PIE?
I WILL HAVE THE OTHER HALF

A pork pie
Cut it in half
Jelly inside
Where is the meat?
It's gone to hide
No egg or cranberry bits
Eat it by the used by date
If you don't, it might give you the s---s
Only joking, pork pies are nice
As I said, cut it in half
You can eat it twice
A pastry outer
Sausage on the inside
Yummy and scrumptious
"Do you think you are getting the other half?"
"Don't be presumptuous"
Ideal for buffets at parties
Eat one as a snack
Pork pies were a favourite of grandad's
"Go to the shop son"
"Fetch us a pork pie"
"Don't forget the horserace bets"
On my return, grandad said
"Did you put on the bets?"
"Yes" I said
"Where is the pork pie?"
"Did you forget?"
"No, they hadn't got any"
"Instead, I bought you some cigarettes".

2013 August
Thursday 15

THE WHITE GATE

The tree of life
Is made for one
Spread those wings
From thy root
Pass life and multiply
One then becomes many
And soon to equal balance
Be born, then become the shadow
A shadow of dust
Wait and be waited on
At the white gate.

August 2013
16 Friday

ART IN MOTION

Fresh as the air that binds the soul
Breathe in life at the potter's wheel
Smooth hands bring a shape to life
A jug or cup to intake water
To live, survive
Art in the clay piece
Makes life come alive
To carry on
Make, create, live
Breathe life
Form takes shape
Objects which you desire
Turning the wheel
Energy forced through the foot
A peddling motion
A rhythmic process
Breathing life into the piece
Life in the potter's hands
Art in motion.

2013 August
Saturday 17

WHAT AM I GOING TO WRITE TODAY?

Time's running out
For the words to flow
Might have to knock it on the head
Never mind today
What am I going to write tomorrow?
No magic from the mind to the pen
The bin is full of screwed up paper
I will have to empty it soon and start again
Why can't I think of something to say?
I would have wrapped this verse up earlier
If I'd had my way.

Sunday 18

WHAT AM I GOING TO WRITE TOMORROW?

The same as yesterday
What am I going to write today?
All this confusion
What's with this word drought
My mind's fighting to find
The togetherness of letters
I can't hear it shout
What am I going to write tomorrow?
Maybe a long poem
Like Dante's Divine comedy
Or maybe nothing, slang, nout.

August 2013
19 Monday

HORRIBLE BOB

Horrible Bob lives next door
He's our favourite slob
Bob's overweight he's not thin anymore
A professional hoarder
His house is full of junk
Mail, TVs and boxes from ceiling to floor
Bob's got varicose veins
They look like blue cords
How can he find his way through that muck?
If he's not careful he will turn into that junk
If he gets stuck
With his weight and all that rubbish
No wonder he finds it hard to move around
I think his head is definitely in the clouds
But horrible Bob used to be thin
He had a beautiful wife
Who was in love with him
She died of the horrible C
This turned Bob into the horrible B
As we could see
Becoming a hoarder is a 24-hour job
So the moral of this story is
If the boxes are stacked high
Knock them down
Your fall from grace
No shame or disgrace
Build your own box inside
Don't let them tumble and fall
Clean the house and mind
Get rid of the hoard
Start afresh, become brand new
Throw away the hurt and the boxes
Turn into a new you
It's never too late!

2013 August
Tuesday 20

MY DUST SAND

A crawling, striking, desolate sand
Flow into the oasis at dark night
Camel trail, prints are many
The fear of a lost soul
Alone, cold, withered, burnt face
A little trace of water from the leather drinking purse
To survive the desert is to choose to die
A burden of choice
Winds are raised
Quietness is lost
Lost is the day
Darkness breaks the camel's back
The fear will end soon
Left to become bones
A personal, torturing death
Soon to rest in the sand
Becoming part of that vast golden desert
Water has gone
Days and months pass
Death is upon me
What is at hand?
My dust sand.

August 2013
21 Wednesday

BLANK

Blank, blank, blank
I am that soldier in that virtual tank
At war, in another world
Blank, blank, blank
I am that policeman
On the beat
A Sergeant is my rank
Blank, blank, blank
I am that child in the bath
Where my toy battleship sank
Blank, blank, blank.

2013 August
Thursday 22

BLANK TOO

I am that builder
Laying bricks on the trestles and planks
Blank, blank, blank
I was that drunk
The beer I drank
Blank, blank, blank
I am the poet who is trying to fill in all those blanks
Trying for perfection
My heart has dropped
The noise was a clank
Use the brain
The most powerful computer of them all
Use the mind to finish this poem
The end is a blank.

August 2013
23 Friday

OUR BET

A special lady was a friend of humour and trust
A family to bring upon this world
Her sons, their sons, a, granddaughter, a little girl
A love is lost, but only in sight
She of love and peace, her spirit still remains
A real smile is now upon her face
In heaven with her husband
This is her place, memories
Many in a book that binds
That journey is a book of the powerful mind
She, who will never be forgotten
These people will never forget
Her family, friends, me
That's our Bet.

2013 August
Saturday 24

A TRAPPED SOUL

Punches are thrown
Tempers full speed
Young, testosterone, Neanderthals
An enraged animal held down
Trying to escape his eternal cage
All that squealing and rage
He looks like a fool
Trying to break the number 1 rule
Losing control
Other men have him in a hold
A trapped soul.

Sunday 25

T.E.O.T.L

A drawer is pushed
A drawer is pulled
Drawers are worn
Sometimes a score draw
Withdraw your cash
From the hole in the wall
Draw a picture of a poem
Draw blood with a needle
Draw a line from the start to the end
--------------------- the end of the line!!

August 2013
26 Monday

PLAY WITH WORDS

Let the cat out of the bag
Pull the rabbit from the hat
See the man about the dog
But don't lose your rag
Let the chicken cross the road
To see the frog and toad
There's bats in the belfry
Wise monkeys, there are three
Let the dog see the rabbit
Let the fish see the chips
Let Jonah inside the whale
Let Noah build the ark
So the flood can be conquered
The animals were two by two
Let the porter see the loo
A mishmash of sayings
A gathering of gibberish in words
Written down, read out in a roundabout way
Just another play with words.

2013 August
Tuesday 27

A GLIMPSE OF PARADISE

But it is of weakness that we stumble upon
A long awaited strength
Disregarding everything
I can sniff out, find and knock on strength's door
Welcome, master one has arrived
Come in, take your shoes off because of the floor,
Freedom awaits a certain kind of person
It is drawn upon them quicker than their counterparts
Flying like a fighter jet, right there
People with big hearts, patience, courage and determination
A good start, a field of dreams, attractive thoughts
Waiting to feel our feet in the fine, lush, blades of green grass
Flavouring smells one could only describe
As a comparison of fragrance from a beautiful woman
A piece of Heaven calls, fades and falls
A glimpse of paradise.

August 2013
28 Wednesday

THE MENU OF WAR

A quiet fog, shooter's breath
Rifles lay beside their owners
War, a grey colour
A somewhat disturbing shade
Possession or freedom for religion
Death is more like the catch of the day
Most popular on the menu
A list of destruction
Death chosen by most
Send it back, it tastes rotten
Feelings of guilt ridden horror
Evilness in gargantuan amounts
Tragic sights, worn, war torn limbs
Bloody displaced bones and flesh
Where they should not be
Exploding mines
Change the lives of both sides
Bullets lodged, shrapnel wounds
Dished out like a dessert
From the menu of war
Politicians with dirty hands
Blood remains in their bodies
Not spilled out like a soldier's red liquid
Blooded scars deeply encroached
Into their digits
The guns slip through
Their so called leader's fingers
Playing that same tune again Sam
Change the menu of war
Will our food taste good again?
Can we all eat in peace!

2013 August
Thursday 29

A LITTLE ONE

A little one
Pride and joy
Girl or boy
A bundle of love
Children, special, pure
An adult's happiness
A tonic and cure
A life of fun and joy
Girl or boy
A little one.

August 2013
30 Friday

RIOT IN MY MIND

The eyes awake
Days start with a thought
Subjects, ideas crossing my mind
Struggling to find peace
Recklessness, trauma disengaging the brain
Termites tearing through the head
As their energy creates a mystical fog
Call on the executioner
Invite the head to the axe
Stop all the words floating in and all around
Call the head police, ring 999
To stop the riot in my mind!!!

2013 August
Saturday 31

TAKE THE CLOUDS AWAY

What have we left to see?
If we take the clouds away
Just blue skies
Light and still
Calmness and sunlight
Sky blue bright
Take the clouds away
No rain for that sunny day
Clouds, white, light and fluffy
Picturesque, in need of a frame
Frame the day
Make it perfect
In a serine special way
Is the weather that predictable?
Sun, rain, wind and snow
It comes, goes, stays and leaves again
Work, rest and play
A certainty, we can't take the clouds away.

SEPTEMBER 2013

2013 September
Sunday 1

THE WORLD CAN WAIT

Why does the world weigh down the shoulders?
Can it weigh down the feet?
Walk out onto the street
The world is outside with its coat on
Taking hits from the cold
Stress, sometimes bold
Pressures at boiling point
Cardiac arrest, pains in the chest
Calm yourself down
Relax, wipe away that frown
Don't let frustration become your friend
Please yourself, live as you want to live
Don't hesitate, a time, a place, a date
The world can wait.

September 2013
2 Monday

GO ON, WRITE A BOOK

Write a book if you can
Fiction or non-fiction
A thriller, play or song
Write a short story
They're not too long
Maybe a children's book
Make a few bob
If money comes rolling in
What a nice job
Go around the globe
Write about your travels
Have a go at writing a self-help book
To unravel the misfortunes in people's lives
A book about affairs
Husbands and wives
Books are exciting
Books are fun
You don't know where they will lead you
To the end, I should imagine
Pardon the pun.

2013 September
Tuesday 3

PAY FOR THE RIGHT TRAIN

That's the last train to Ruinville
I'm glad I missed it
Nearly had a first class ticket
Quickly got off at the right station
Fragmentation, not my jurisdiction
The boiler room was stoked
Not to remain provoked
Hardly a word passed through the lips
A death wish kiss
Trouble artificially breaking one's head
A real presence of misfortune
A distant player of fortune
Nothing gained, nothing squandered
Something I am fond of
Take control, will power
On a roll to Jerusalem
Hallelujah
Pay for the right train.

September 2013
4 Wednesday

POLTERBAG

The bag moves
Like a ghost in the room
A face appears through the white plastic
A horror film in a bag
The face like rubber
Stretched elastic
Polterbag fantastic
Scary movie, don't make me laugh
This was real, you don't know the half
A biodegradable bag
Nice to the environment
I don't think so
Smiles are not glad
Haunting to see
Polterbag in the room
One, two and the ghost makes three
All of a sudden, the bag goes flat
The rubber faced spirit has gone
Maybe the bag has left the room for the shopping
Moved to another carrier
The ghoul is plastic bag hopping.

2013 September
Thursday 5

SYD BARRETT WITHOUT A BIKE

A potent trip, a bit of a slip
Cut to the diamond in the rough
The bike chained up
The owner has gone
Magic is still there
The Octopus flies
A shining light
The edge of the gem
Shines through the eye
I am waiting
Are we there yet?
On our own
But with a mother to boot
Tormented soul
Freudian like
Like Syd Barrett
Without the bike.

September 2013
6 Friday

NO MORE

No more shit
No more stress
Think about yourself for a change
Not the rest, I can't do that
The gutter calls
Fall at the wayside
Flat on your face
Get back up
Don't leave a trace
Boxing gloves are on
Battling every day
Hoping the gutter is far, far away
The gutter draws you back
Trying to make you part of its concrete family
I don't want the curb to be my brother
Look at the other side of the road
Where the grass is greener
It's a softer landing to the floor
The gutter remains a distant memory
No more, no more, no more.

2013 September
Saturday 7

SHOES ARE TIGHT

Shoes are tight
Hard times we tread
Tired feet, tired legs
Take it easy
Take a seat
Too much work
Brings tired feet.

Sunday 8

TIGHTEN YOUR BELT

Mind your money
Tighten your belt
Money fades, Benjamin Franklin
Money falls, Isaac Newton
The Dollar, the Pound
It can take you up
Push you to the ground
Does it make it go round?

September 2013
9 Monday

GO TO FREEDOM

When faith is at a loss
Turn to hope as your back up
Walk to the train
Roll down the tracks
Buy that ticket to freedom
Find your destination
Mind the doors
P.S
And the gap.

2013 September
Tuesday 10

THE COIN IN THE HAT

Inside the pockets
A change will come
Spend wisely with thy coin
A last penny dropped
Into the busker's hat
Filled to the brim
Of the inch and a half brown coloured fedora hat
Sometimes enough to feed for a week
I'm glad to say, so to speak
Someone in need, seems to please
Satisfaction, a smile from both
The chord is played
The coin is flipped
He who helped me, with the tune he played
A joy to the ears
It made my day
The week had passed
Digging deep into my pockets
To hear a tune
The old man had gone to Heaven from song
No longer there, where he played and sat
All that remained was the coin in the hat!

September 2013
11 Wednesday

SLAVE TO A POEM

A slave to life
The mask it hides
Questionable doubts
Routine an addiction
Inflicted upon oneself
No one should be a slave
Slave trade, items are made
Slave to life
Slave to a husband and wife
Slave trade, slave at roots
Slave, slave, slave
Bury this word
Attend slave's funeral
Take it to its grave
Slave to life, who said so?
Routine, why follow?
Slave trade, the poor condemned again
More freedom, give them a raise
Husbands and wives
Slaves to each other
Share and love
Not slave and love
Slave at roots, a despicable time
Holes in clothes and boots
Not a nice life
Abolish slavery in all forms
Except in this poem!

2013 September
Thursday 12

A DAY, A YEAR, A LIFE

A day comes
Finishes when it ends
A week of pictures
Eyes look through the lens
Months pass by
As quick as a storm
That bites cold to the face
Years to years
Many shall pass
Bringing sadness
Bringing gladness
Some a waste
Some a Heavenly life
Smiles for the few
Torment at most
A new year, a new time
A new life
Time to live
With time, you won't catch up
Until time stops.

September 2013
13 Friday

THE DOOR IS FIRMLY BOLTED

Trace a picture on a page
Retrace your tracks
Decipher the mind
Plans are made
Think, teach, train
A torrential stormy brain
Five, six, maybe seven stories at once
Colliding, grasping, a workout
An aerobic of thoughts
Don't get caught my son
Do not let him in
He who comes knocking
Don't find it shocking
If he turns to the bell
Do not sell
Do not buy either
Into a false, laid down pair of hands
Listen to the prayer
Not to the red tongued evil stare
Bolt that door to the mind tight
All days and every night.

2013 September
Saturday 14

THE GOOD LIFE HAS COME

Divineness comes after a shadow of a doubt
Box the ring, in thy bout
Shout out loud to the Gods at will
Stirring, courageous, strong emotions
Make it a magical potion of positivity
Is it rife?
Welcome to the good life.

Sunday 15

HAS IT ALWAYS BEEN THERE?

Lying dormant
That was the torment
All those years
A waist of tears
A lot to bear
The good life for the future
Has it always been there?

September 2013
16 Monday

P.S

She of the night
Cool, white and black
A natural light
Through the mist and fog
Rock and roll angel
Side saddles her horse
Free and alive
A patron of the poetry world
An oath to the truth
Sing bird sing
Jesus within the walls of her heart
Beating loud, always heard
Just the kid at the Chelsea
Her art passes on
To everyone and me
Her music, raw, rolls along
A burst of energy finishes the score
Dark sunglasses on
Rolling to the tune
Of the heavenly white winged horse
The poet keeper now rides Pegasus!

2013 September
Tuesday 17

BRAIN COMPUTER

Discrepancies from above
Cleanse one's thoughts
To a shade, a white dove
The horse has wings
Distant memories finally pass
The angel now sings on a forceful plain
To regain freedom
A kind of militant peace
Where's my receipt?
I want a refund on peace
Sacrifices are made
The head to the pillow is laid
A repeat of destruction, in thought
Rears its ugly head once more
A virtual language of words
Floats in and drops the bomb
Take it away, please be gone
Clear the browsing history
From the biggest computer of them all
To the brain we call.

September 2013
18 Wednesday

LET COMEDY IN

Comedy, humour, laughs and fun
Let's hear the pun
Laughter on the face
Raised sound
Bellowing sound
Heckled at ground
A jester's stage
Kings of comedy
Laughing's the remedy
Cracking jokes
Tailored to an audience
As if it were bespoke
Laughs a minute
Audience's approval
You want to win it
A joker to the stage
Sounds of laughter
Released from the cage
Knock, Knock who's there?
There is somebody at the door
Let them in, it's only fair
Through the letter box
I can see a grin
Let comedy in.

2013 September
Thursday 19

T.A.P

An artificial thought
Don't be stupid
They're real you know
An artificial leg
Gives you that get up and go
An artificial official
There's plenty of those
The artificial poet
Poetry and prose
Writes "Life to a rose"
He thinks he's artificial
Hopefully his popularity grows
Snobbery at best
Give it a rest
Poetry is for everyone
Pointing fingers
Pokes his or her nose
The public aren't artificial
They are real
They will tell you what you want to hear
Or not, I suppose.

September 2013
20 Friday

A DESOLATE DESERT ISLAND

Man Friday
Woman Thursday
On a hot desert island
Both very thirsty
Shipwrecked
Lives wrecked
Torn apart
Brought together
Bloody scorching weather
The island is their new home
A least they are not alone
Using their resources
Not many at that
Their real home is far away now
An empty flat
Except for the cat
Stuck on this desert island
Feels like they are on remand
At least man Friday has got woman Thursday
To hold his desperately shaking hand.

2013 September
Saturday 21

1, 2, 3, I FELL --- -- - ---- AGED 5

One, two, three
I fell out of a tree
I landed on my coccyx
Then I ate my Cox's
An apple, that is
Which had fallen next to me
Poor bruised apple
Poor bruised me
1, 2, 3, I fell out of a tree
Aged 5

Sunday 22

SUNDAY AGAIN

Sunday again
Goes so quick
Getting tired
Slow as a brick
Should be a good week
Hopefully, so to speak
We will see
When it's Sunday again
At the end of the working week.

September 2013
23 Monday

KEEP LOVE IN MIND

To be held in one's arms
A passionate fate
An imaginary expedition of love
If reality finds it, then great
For a few, it's there
For others, not
But time will pass on
And time will stop
To find her, some mean feat
Get off your seat
Don't give up
The look for love
Hand to a glove
A bond that fits
The wedding in church
The candle is lit
Vows are made
Trust is upon them
Throughout their days
Don't regret the time you have had
The good times, the bad
The happy and sad
Just keep love in mind.

2013 September
Tuesday 24

TIME IS YOURS

At fast pace
Slow down
Have a break
Relax, find the time
Be at peace
Try to unwind
Then you might find
Quality of life
Tension released
Please yourself
Time is yours.

September 2013
25 Wednesday

FINALLY, I HAVE ARRIVED

I'm here at last
Is that Peter?
Will he let me past?
A fulfilled life
Or maybe not
A long walk from the gates
Where to next?
White feathers malting behind me
Is that what I think it is?
The garden of Eden tree
Looks like Heaven
I imagine it to be
Feels like Heaven
Could it be?
Is it Heaven?
Bread unleavened
Wine tasted as I go
No one in sight
Just as I thought
Wait, in the distance
A solitary figure
Could it be God?
Whoosh, something is close
A most marvellous feeling
A peaceful sound, a quiet breath
A host of calm, tiny steps
Is this Heaven?
Don't be absurd
Fly and be free
Look at me I'm a bird
Finally, I have arrived.

2013 September
Thursday 26

A QUICK GLIMPSE

Head and body is on fire
Sold your soul, liar, liar
Seething, sinister, trepidation
What am I doing here?
Surely this isn't my station
I want the elevator up
Not the escalator down
Who is that close up?
In my face, lizard frown
Fear times infinity
Holy trinity Batman
No time for humour
At a time like this
My blood, it drains like a sieve
What is this?
Tutivillus, surely not
I wake up
Haven't been there since
I hope Heaven is calling
Was this a warning?
A quick glimpse.

September 2013
27 Friday

A GOOD HOLIDAY

Travelling light
Small case in hand
The world is waiting
Rain, sun or sand
A mixture of cultures
A breath of fine air
Sounds and lights
New clothing to wear
Feelings of freedom
Rejuvenating thoughts
Fun and happiness
Trinkets are bought
Many delights
Food and music
Drinking and dancing
Time for romancing
Sun across the market place
Lounging, relaxing
Sun coloured face
Time to chill, read a book
Visiting ruins, take a look
Touring around, castles and old towns
Swim in the sea, a dip in the pool
In the shade, keeping cool
Waiter service, drinks on a tray
Just a few things
That make a good holiday.

2013 September
Saturday 28

THE GIRL

The girl is shy
I wonder why?
Too pretty to pass by
A twinkle in her eye
Her long, shiny hair
A smile without a care
Like a china doll toy
She impresses this boy.

Sunday 29

TAKE THE STEPS

Today's the day to have your say
Tomorrow is key for your future
Take the steps
Open the door
Greatness might come into your life
A thought, a feeling, a child, a husband or wife
Connect with the day that is upon you
Make it yours, own it, see it through
No steps taken, you will stand still
Strive for life at your own will
Take the steps, life is there to fulfil.

September 2013
30 Monday

THE WORLD IS YOURS

Destination, where are you going?
Walking, driving, flying or rowing
Walking, taking one's time
Driving, getting further down the line
Fly across the world, life is yours
Maybe row, for a good cause
All in all
You will get to where you are going
Travel and unravel
Life in other cities
Other towns, life around the world
Up and down, the globe is yours
To discover at will
Don't leave it too late
When you're over the hill
Life around the globe
The world is yours for the taking.

OCTOBER 2013

October 2013
1 Tuesday

SHE IS MY LIFE

She seems pretty easy to please
She knows my traits
She knows my love and hates
She holds me like an angel
She is my one and only
With her I'm never lonely
A woman of peace and passion
With me she's always in fashion
She, a warm hearted lover
With her, one will discover
Many different things to life
She always seems to surprise
She of long hair and brown eyes
A husband and a wife
She is my everything
She is my wife.

2013 October
Wednesday 2

MY HAIR POEM

Hair grows, longer and longer
Before you know
It's out of control
It looks a mess
Something one needs to address
The locks are scruffy
Smarten it up
Go to the barbers
Get the thing cut
Hair getting thin
Going grey
Growing at speed
In the natural way
I wouldn't dye it
I'd look like a fool
Anyway, I think the grey looks cool
So, a short to medium cut
Suits me just fine
How long do you leave it?
Where do you draw the line?
People who cut hair
Will never run out of trade
Unless people cut their own hair
But then errors will be made.

October 2013
3 Thursday

LET THE FOX FLEE

As foxes flee
Night time closes in
Away from our world of darkness
Beware of the fox
Sly thoughts, inside the box
Creeping towards a mind
Full of destruction
Decomposing brain matter
The fox has gone
Broken and shattered
Nightmares all round
Sweat stained nightshirt
Tremors, breathlessness
Badness lurks, beyond the universe
Let the fox into the cold
No more curse.

NIGHT TIME ADVENTURES

Children, readers of the night
Trusted, misjudged
Help is at hand
Surprised by delight
Journey to the promised land
Children of the night
The tent cover is made
Torch light shining
A magical journey
Toys with children
Bert and Ernie
Magical worlds, imaginations
Busy and bold
Round the globe
Navigation is their role
The Far East, the outback
Arabian nights
Running through the market towns
Saving the beautiful girl
In the hot air balloon
Across Europe's great cities
Batteries have gone
What a pity
A back up torch
So the child can read and look
All those exciting stories
Through the world of books
Night time adventures.

October 2013
5 Saturday

KEEP THE PAGES TURNING

Genuine concern
When you can't grasp to learn
Keep reading through
This will benefit you
Go over the words again
Learning is your gain
Education for the young
Keeping a healthy brain
Train at an early age
Studying, keep turning the page.

6 Sunday

TEA TO UNWIND

Tea or not to be tea
Would you like a cup?
Get the biscuits
Have a dunk
Chocolate covered
Garibaldi too
Take a break
Maybe a Kit-Kat for you
Chill out and unwind
Put your feet up
Later on, maybe have another cup.

2013 October
Monday 7

SHOOTING A MOVIE

A hired gun takes his time
His mark is seen
Takes the shot
The target wiped out clean
Cool as Bond
Not shaken, not stirred
Sirens are echoing
The hitman flees the scene
The getaway, like a shadow
As if it were a dream
Police everywhere
Security alert
Mayhem on the streets
People getting hurt
It will take time to catch this shooter
If they ever will
An investigation
Clues are there to find and see
Mind you, these are just some words
Describing a thrilling crime movie.

October 2013
8 Tuesday

A BUTTON ON A JACKET

A button on a jacket
Do your coat up
Leave it open
Too cold for that
Fasten all the buttons
Right up to the neck
Keep the cold out
Look out the window
For a weather check
If the button drops off
Sow it back on
Unless you lose it
Then it will be gone
Probably have a spare
So don't you threat
Replace it with a needle
And piece of cotton thread
Big buttons, small buttons
Colourful at that
Most buttons are round
Like a head for a hat
The button becomes redundant
When it's a zip
No more talking on this page
So, I'm going to button it.

2013 October
Wednesday 9

T.N.T

The day in today
Is partnered with a to
So is to with day
Today's the day
Today is now
Have a good day
But if you don't
Do not dismay
There is always tomorrow
If that's bad, then there's the next
Why do I keep writing today in this text?
Can't I change today?
It's getting on my nerves
Maybe put tomorrow in this rhyming verse
But then it could be like today
Tomorrow could be worse
At least the T tomorrow and the T today
Will quench our thirst.

October 2013
10 Thursday

OUR HUMAN RACE

Beside myself
Awash with hate
Injustice in bounds
Stop the creation
Flee from the scene
Fight for justice
Scrub the hate clean
Oppression, depression, suppression
Respiratory recession
A mad world, a struggle at that
Most in tow, trailing behind
Beaten down from time to time
Does the system work?
Miley Cyrus, forget the twerk
Chaos in this world
Is it like this on other planets throughout space?
Or is it just our human race?

2013 October
Friday 11

THE RIGHTEOUSNESS OF EVOLUTION

The Greek Gods look down upon thee
Fortune and destiny
My time is now
To seek is to be found
A certain truth washes in front of my eyes
Fame is close
Happiness is closer
Tragedy has taken a backseat
A modern day Confucius
Carry on the work
Learn and pass on knowledge
Push it under their noses
Educate, let it grow
Make righteousness flow
Today and always
Be free, walk into the sea of Galilee
Come out smelling of roses
Walk onto the land
Grow like the flowers
A rose's scent
Forever hell-bent
For goodness and wellbeing
For all life form.

October 2013
12 Saturday

SECRECY UNFOLDS

A clandestine event takes place
Secret hand shake
Difficult to fake
Above the law
So they think
Business discussed
Discreetness a must
Masks are worn
Capes are Black
Don't get drawn in
Take a seat at the back.

13 Sunday

SECRETS ARE TOLD

The ink on the paper
A secret is told
Passed around
The hand makes the fold
Open for a vote
What's inside the note?
Who rules the world?
The dollar sign is their motto
Obscene is the word
Controlling everyone
Until the big man wipes out the herd.

2013 October
Monday 14

A MISHMASH SEQUEL

A brick to a house
Wine to the glass
A trap caught the mouse
Poor little chap
A roof with a hole
Rain washes in
Sugar in the tea
Pass the biscuits, they are in the cake tin
The TV's on, watching a movie
My woman's heading into the lounge towards me
She smells nice
Perfume to the nose
She has sandals on
Showing her toes
Blue jeans projecting her perfect shape
We have just eaten our dinner
Two empty plates.

October 2013
15 Tuesday

MY BEDROOM AS A KID

Ten years of age
About my bedroom
On this page
Brown bed covers
Magnolia walls
Sticker books and posters
Leather and sponge footballs
Music is played
Record the charts
Who's at number one
Press play to start
Anaglypta wallpaper
Let's keep to the script yeah
Shared room, brother's in twin
Black and white TV
Watch our team win
Not many reading books
What a shame that was
Saturday morning picture show
Bruce Lee, Godzilla, Tiswas
Happy memories in my bedroom
That's where I slept
After I came out of the womb.

2013 October
Wednesday 16

A TOENAIL CLIPPING

A toenail clipping
Springs off the toe
Sometimes you can't find it
Where does it go?
Cut another nail
Does it follow the same route?
Flies off elsewhere
Get ready to shoot
Not a nice chore
Toenails at length
The tough ones to cut
You will need all your strength
Walking around the house
With no shoes and socks on
A missed toenail, one you forgot
Cuts right into your foot
Strutting your stuff
Now that the nails are trimmed, clipped and clean
Leave your socks off
The feet can be seen
Next is the hard skin
To make soft and pristine.

October 2013
17 Thursday

A FARM

Warm is the night
Long is the day
Straw in the barn
Bundles of hay
Summer on the farm
The graft is hard work
Early mornings
No time to shirk
Cows are milked
The pigs are well fed
Sheep are rounded up
The dog rests his head
In for lunch
The farmhand deserves a brew
So does the farmer
He's done in too
After their break
It's back to the grind
Earn their daily bread
Farm work is hard to find
Summer on the farm
Goes quick as a storm
Rape seed in the one field
Chickens, eggs, wheat and corn
The farmer's work is done, winter sets in
But which time of the year does a farmer begin.

2013 October
Friday 18

PRICES SHOULD BE DOWN

Numbers we count
Add or subtract
Money we earn
Spent or pay tax
Beg, lend or borrow
As long as you don't steal
Cash tills are open
A white receipt reel
A supermarket world
A fortune they make
Raising their costs
Would be a mistake
Prices should be down
Not just to a pound
Make the shopping cheaper
Change things around
Better cheaper deals
Should be in place
Before we eat our meals
Remind us to say grace.

October 2013
19 Saturday

ROAM IN ROME

The penny dropped
A twinkle in the fountain
Hands cold, side by side
Resting on the Spanish steps
A gentle flowing crowd
Voices are silent
Peace and quiet
Not too loud
At this moment in time
I don't miss home
Happy to roam
In this great city that is Rome.

20 Sunday

BRAVE NEW WORLD INDEED

Technology has taken the world by the scruff of the neck
Download the seed
It's a brave new world indeed.

2013 October
Monday 21

POINT THE FINGER

A cuticle in the right direction
Point the finger
Pass on the blame
Human mistakes
There's no shame
Take on your errors
Don't point the finger
Accept faults
We all make them
Even if they are bad
A right stinger
Don't point the finger.

October 2013
22 Tuesday

BLUE AND WHITE

Blue and White
I don't know what to write
I do really
They are my team you see
Birmingham City
A history, 1875
The year they came alive
Dynamite, drive on at will
Blue and White
Number one, keep right on
St Andrews, the Kop, the Tilton
This is our city
There's a light
Keep up the fight
Blue and White.

2013 October
Wednesday 23

A NET

Annette, a girl's name
A net filled with holes
Especially nets for catching fish
On the end of a pole
A tennis court has a net
Sometimes hit with a ball
Are we all caught in one big net ready for the fall?
Net curtains to hide behind for that nosy neighbour
A trapeze artist
The safety net's their saviour
Hair nets in food factories
In case hairs fall out
Insect nets, when there are mosquitoes about
These days, the biggest net of all is electronic communication
It's the Internet of course.

October 2013
24 Thursday

THE TO THE A

The driver manoeuvres onto his drive
A bee sees its hive
The fixer sells the fix
A magician shows his tricks
The criminal commits a crime
The poet recites his rhyme
The policeman nicks the thief
A red Indian calls to his chief
The baby loves its mother
A lover, there is no other
The cross is carried away
A preacher has his say
The rat is a sneak and a cheat
A quiet man is very discreet
The bridge, to get to the other side
A buzz from a theme park ride
The sharks with teeth that cut
A chimney stack that's full of soot
The bark is worse than the bite
A boxer does 12 rounds at the fight
The wave of a hand goodbye
A world to live, breathe and fly.

2013 October
Friday 25

A VARIETY OF WEATHER

Rise to the sky
Let yourself fly
Breeze through the wind and fog
Take the storm by surprise
The rain has to come
So does the sun
When it's too cold, one sighs
The sun warms the heart
A downpour of shade
The rain is hot
The thunder and lightning afraid
Weather that's confused
An umbrella can be used
In the sun or rain
A mixture of weather
In Great Britain
Even the weather in this poem
Is changing while it's being written
There are all kinds of weather, you see
A least there is a variety.

October 2013
26 Saturday

MAKE LIFE GRAND

Near the end
Is it where we finish?
Or is it where we start?
Your world begins
Take the future
In one hand
Make life grand.

27 Sunday

C.G.B

Clocks go back
As quick as a flash
The future tends to soar
Mornings are black
The night comes quick
It's summertime no more.

R.I.P Lou Reed/ Sunday morning.

2013 October
Monday 28

A SPECIAL PERSON

A special person rises up
A special person shares their cup
A special person looks after everyone
A special person is missed when gone
A special person is patient and caring
A special person you know you can trust
A special person will be scattered when they're dust
A special person puts everyone else first
A special person, they're the best, not worst
A special person shows love and helps everyone
A person that's special
Carry on!!!!

October 2013
29 Tuesday

SHREWSBURY TUESDAY

I wonder if it is Tuesday in Shrewsbury?
Or Wednesday in Wednesbury?
It is Tuesday in Shrewsbury
It will be Wednesday in Wednesbury
I once had a bath in Bath
It was a bright one in Brighton
Someone had a chip at me in Chipping Norton
I fell down a ditch in Shoreditch
In Richmond I became rich
It's still Tuesday in Shrewsbury
I think I lost my marbles by Marble Arch.

2013 October
Wednesday 30

HALLOWEEN EVE

It's time, we are nearly there
The ghosts and ghouls will share
Their scary haunts, night and day
No, fright and day
The shadows of darkness
Rise from the crypt
Are we ready?
What's next in this script?
The pumpkins are carved
Candles are alight
Trick or treat?
Into the dark night
The next night will come
Halloween, the kids will be out
Costumes are seen
Dish out the tricks
Goodies they receive
The night before Halloween
It's Halloween Eve.

October 2013
31 Thursday

SPOOKY TIMES

Ghouls and ghosts
Spiders on toast
Witches on broomsticks
Treat or tricks
Bubbling cauldrons
Newts and toads
Zombies and werewolves
Darkened roads
Pumpkins and lights
Black cloaks
White as a ghost
The gnawing rat
The vampire bat
Crossing the path
Here comes the black cat
Wooing sounds
Clinking from the grave
Dracula's bite
Frankenstein's there to fright
Mummies are wrapped
Spooky rhymes
For spooky times.

NOVEMBER 2013

November 2013
1 Friday

A QUIET PLACE

Go to the quiet place
It's a different race
Where the angels go
They dance to the light
It's one fantastic show
Reaping rewards
That have never been seen
Only in dreams, you will see
Send in the dream maker
He's no fake
Take and be taken
Into the peaceful, quiet night
Where we all shall sing
Seeking eternal light
Get things off your chest
Go to the quiet place
Be at peace and rest
Relaxed eyes, relaxed mind
Bodies are cool
A restful, hypnotic sign
Saving fate, saviours grace
A quiet place.

2013 November
Saturday 2

FOOD FOR EVERYONE

From the flames he rose
From the soil it grows
Vegetables, flowers, grass
Organic things grow
Rain shall pass
Sunlight upon this earthly world
No one should go hungry
Not today or ever
Food forever
For everyone.

Sunday 3

AT THE END OF THIS BOOK

At the end of the book
There's a bind
At the start of the book
You will find
A story to be read, many lines
A book to educate mankind
When you have read this book
I hope it was worth the time it took
Hoping a chord will be struck
When you get to the end of this book.

November 2013
4 Monday

THE NIGHT BEFORE THE FIRE

The plot was at hand
A torch ready to light
1605! years later became bonfire night
The House of Lords, in the cellar
A failed assassination against James the 1st
King of England and VI of Scotland
Guy Fawkes, in charge of explosives
A military man found guarding 36 barrels of gunpowder
Foiled was their plan
The gunpowder plot shot down in flames
The flames still remain, tomorrow the 5th, bonfire night again
Robert Catesby and the rest were shot or hanged.

2013 November
Tuesday 5

LET THE FIREWORKS BEGIN

The fireworks are ready
Penny for the Guy
Children waving sparklers
The bonfire is stacked high
Rockets and Catherine wheels
Bangers and baked spuds
Everybody cosy
Hats, scarves and gloves
Lights and noise
Fun for the kids
Let the fireworks begin
On November the 5th

November 2013
6 Wednesday

SWEEP THE DUST AWAY

Just dust on the ground
Not much sound
The bonfire is out
Litter is cleared
Until next year's fire
52 weeks to the day
For now
Sweep the dust away.

2013 November
Thursday 7

EVERY FACE HAS A TELL

The lines show
What can we sell?
Our thoughts of wisdom
Every face has a tell
What's inside?
Evil or Saint
A blank canvas
Pictures to paint
The story unfolds
An unnerving fear
Keep your loved ones close
The angels are here
Behind the eyes
The tissue attached
All cards are dealt
Hands to catch
What's on your mind?
Does anyone know?
Stern poker face
Does it show?
The muscles relax
A raised eyebrow
Can we know?
If not, then how?
Look deep through their soul
To the depths of hell
The game is yours
Every face has a tell.

November 2013
8 Friday

TURN THE MEAN TO CLEAN

A road to freedom
Has come and gone
The lyrics are written
From heart to song
Cut the strings son
Make her yours
Take her and hold her
Forever more
Don't be afraid
Say what you mean
They will have to listen
Turn the mean to clean.

2013 November
Saturday 9

THE EDGE OF REASON

Beholden to life
What's in store next?
Youth fades
Wisdom for some approaches
It will come
A change of season
When we are on
The edge of reason.

Sunday 10
Remembrance Sunday

REMEMBER THOSE WHO GAVE US OUR FUTURE

A country to be proud of
Heroes, yesteryear and present
Fought, died, sacrificed their lives
Making way for ours
Protecting the people of our nation
With no hesitation
Remember those who gave us our future.

November 2013
11 Monday

A MISHMASH TRILOGY

Washing in Washington
Drying in Dresden
Stoking the fire in Stoke
Growing cress at Cressington Station
Something new in New York
Eating Yorkies in Yorkshire
Winding down in Windermere
Speaking to Mary in Maryland
Swaying in Swaziland
Building a bridge in Bridgnorth
Pole dancing in Poland
Living by a pool in Liverpool
Writing poems on a pad in Paddington
Shopping in a shop in Shropshire
Eyes are smiling in Ireland
Is everything new in Newtown?
It's not toxic in Toxteth
Is there a lot of moss in Moss Side?
Drinking a Bordeaux in Bordeaux
Wearing burgundy in Burgundy
A Parisian in Paris
Being us in the USA
Finishing this poem in Finland
Ending in England.

2013 November
Tuesday 12

A ROAD

Black and white stripes
A road to fame
An insect with no shoes and socks on
Only two remain
An iconic cover
Accents the same
Spaced strides with the foot
Flowing along a winding road
No it's curb to curb
I'm not sleeping
Do not disturb
The other side is waiting
Just one direction
On a quiet road
Frog and toad
The zebra crossing has a name
A road.

November 2013
13 Wednesday

JOINED

Reason within reason
Torment within trust
Why are countries so jaded?
Within reason we adjust
Harmony should be in place
Eventually a sound
Voices heard from within
Bet the dollar to the pound
Big countries across the pond
We keep close by
With all the world's countries joined together
We could reach our Heavenly sky.

2013 November
Thursday 14

HOW COULD SOMEONE EVEN CONSIDER DOING THAT TO ANOTHER HUMAN BEING?

Tragic losses
At such a cost
Bombed out
Built back up
Time to reflect
Hurt and chaos
With spirit and victory
So say us
A narcissistic power
Bodies are gassed
A disgusting, despicable atrocity
Can they forget?
Will it pass?
Years of hurt and pain
Struck down like rabid animals
Will they ever feel the same again?
A collection of thoughts
Too many at that
Evil within evil
Under his hat
Lives destroyed
Years of mental torture
You bet they are annoyed
This we shouldn't be seeing
How could someone even consider doing that to
another human being?

November 2013
15 Friday

SPACECRAFT

Sightings of UFO'S
Just below the clouds
Extra terrestrial
Seen from the road
Eyes are deceived
An intake of breath
Is this a dream?
I'm becoming a mess
Aliens on board
Could this be true?
Lights shining down
Blinded by an incandescent light
Streams so bright
To this day I can't seem to get on
What did the spaceship take?
When the craft was forever gone
Me!!!!!!!!!!!!!!!!!!!!!!!!!!!!!!!!!!!!!

2013 November
Saturday 16

TV LICENCE FEE

TV dinners
Michael Winner
Adverts on tap
A film ending
That's a wrap
Too many channels to choose from
More commercials that sell
For all of us to see
The BBC
Pay your licence fee.

Sunday 17

BURNT

Burnt up
Burnt down
Burnt out
Burnt town
Burnt fingers
Burnt sound
Burnt and drowned.

November 2013
18 Monday

THE SCHOOL DREAM

That dream again
Pops its head up
Now and then
Back at school
No clothes on
Use the pencil and rule
Erase the dream
From the mind
The school dream
Bad as it is
Always seems to find
Am I still in detention?
After all these years
Leave behind
All of those fears
School's not in my text book
Change the syllabus
Before it gets stuck
Was it as bad as it seems?
Yes, quick, wake up from the school dream.

2013 November
Tuesday 19

SNOW COVERED CHRISTMAS

The cold nose
A cold face
Whitened winter roads
Fingers in gloves
Scarves around necks
A snowball thrown
An icy patch
Red coloured sledge
Christmas trees
Snow covered hedge
Frosted windows
Candles alight
Look at the decorations through the stained glass
Baubles twinkling so bright
Carol singers in fine voice
Christmas time, a heavenly choice
Children making angels in the snow
Snowmen rolling beginning to grow
Front doors with holly, tinsel and bells
Santa's coming
Ho, ho, ho he yells.

November 2013
20 Wednesday

OF PEACE

Sitting, lying, thinking
A peaceful state of mind
Kind, tranquil thoughts gather
Smooth, slow, drifting thoughts
Moving along in a meditated state
Choose the path of peace
Comfort in being able to concentrate
Your pulse beats along
Like a fined tuned piano
Peace today
Of peace tomorrow
Peace in our time
Peace in our mind
At peace with our body
A moment to cease
When we are in a state of peace.

2013 November
Thursday 21

THE ROAD ALONG THE WAY

Cannot sleep
Holes along the road
A lollipop of yellow in the distance
Escapism from that heavy load
The children crossing
Off to learn their lesson
A passing beat
A passing of time
More potholes
Worn out feet that are mine
Slabbed pavements are cracked
Raised, loose ends
In need of a fix
Throw some sand and cement into the mix
Different sounds of feet
Coughing, sneezing, people meeting
Blue, grey, green
Brick coloured tones
Inside and outside of one's seeing and thinking
Ant like people carrying on as if nothing can change
Why don't they have their say?
On their road, along the way.

November 2013
22 Friday

A GREAT FRIDAY NIGHT

Beauty inside the door
Floor to floor class
Marble, expensive wood and glass
Cocktail glasses at head height
Chinking of cutlery
Outside, a dark night
Waiters, barmaids
Gorgeous women
Dresses that show their shape
Fine cuisine eaten off fine china plates
An array of sporadic noise
Exquisite smells from the kitchen
A good night for the boys
Laughter and fun
Gets the job done
A great Friday night.

2013 November
Saturday 23

SANTA'S THE HOST

It's drawing close
For the kids
Santa's the host
Little faces
Excitement within
A magical time
Their faces wearing a grin.

Sunday 24

POEM FOR THE KIDS

Thomas the tank
His heart sank
When he heard a clank
He crashed his tank
Thomas went to the bank
To withdraw money
To pay for a new tank
Poor Thomas the tank.

November 2013
25 Monday

A THEASAURUS

The smell of an old page
A dusty, smoky scent
Inside this old book
A multitude of words
Jumping out of the page
Springing to mind
Finding meanings
Relating to the words
The English language in fine verse
A writer's best friend
A companion for all of us
The book I am looking at is a thesaurus.

2013 November
Tuesday 26

THAT'S SOME MEAN FEAT

Possibilities are endless
Within the whole world
Every single person has got at least one thing in common
Born naked, strip it down, think deeply about it
Some of us are clowns
Clothes are worn, then the trouble can start
Uniforms are worn
Either destruction or heart
Soldiers put on their gear
War, there is always that fear
Nurses put on their sky blues
There to help
Politicians wear their suits
There's that sigh and a yelp
Terrorists put on their masks
Sometimes a backpack
This is where things end up
Ruin and rack
If we were all naked, stripped down, vulnerable
Would we all be at peace?
That's some mean feat.

November 2013
27 Wednesday

JUSTIN ASHFORD

Just thinking what to write down here
Under my nose or ear
Staring at the page, **it's** clear
Trying to make something appear
Imagine a poem starts with my dear
Nothing is coming close or near
As I look upon the page with fear
Singing a song with love can create a tear
Has my mind gone into another stratosphere?
Float back down to earth with an idea
Out of writing could I make a career?
Round the corner, I will get there if I steer
Drop everything and go for a beer!

2013 November
Thursday 28

A WOMAN WITH CHOICE

An elegant frame
A woman with choice
Tragedy inside
You can hear it in her voice
She knows how to work a room
Mouths are on the floor
Transparent to some
But unclear to most
Drinks are poured
To start the toast
Is she happy?
All this beauty bestowed upon her
Reels and reels of film
The photographer is there to capture
A stunning silhouette
The light fades in the picture
A perfect face, no sign of ageing
At this moment, no trace
This model uses her face as her voice
Beauty, a powerful attribute to have
A woman with choice.

November 2013
29 Friday

LOOK AFTER YOUR PLANET

Earth, our round globe
Home to human beings
A world of different cultures
Climates, vast deserts
Surrounded mainly by water
How many of the population look after their planet?
Is it half, nothing or maybe a quarter?

2013 November
Saturday 30

AN INLET OF HOPE

Not a day goes by
That I think of you
Today's smile is tomorrow's hope
Trading one's truth to another
So I can cope
A person missed
Is a person lost?
Torment comes at such a cost
Some return, a few remain
A special thought from the grave
Look deep into the future
What can you see?
For some reason
I don't think it will be me
Do I be brave and weather the storm?
One day the sun will come
A light will form
To this day I will never forget
An inlet of hope
An inlet of hope.

DECEMBER 2013

2013 December
Sunday 1

A DARK FIGURE

A dark figure walks upon this earth
A dark drink in a light glass
Mystery surrounds him
A certain gravitas
Who or what is he?
They can't work it out
Doesn't seem to be from around this town
What comes to mind is a sore thumb
Should we stay?
Should we run?
No need for a notice or a sign
Plenty of witnesses
There's no crime
A dark figure
Don't try and figure him out
All you need to know is
He's got some clout
Sticks in your mind
Not easy to forget
You can approach him
He won't get upset
Just don't push his trigger
A dark figure.

December 2013
2 Monday

IN A BLINK OF AN EYE

In a blink of an eye
More of life passes by
Life flies like an eagle
Up through the sky
Quicker and quicker
Faster and faster
In a blink of an eye
As more of life's lessons pass us by
Too many thoughts and emotions
In the blink of an eye
Distant memories
Fond and mournful
Years and years pass by
In the blink of an eye
One day, we will all pass by
Eyes will be shut tight
No blink of an eye.

2013 December
Tuesday 3

SOLD DOWN THE RIVER

Sold down the river
A love not lost
Sold to the highest bidder
A slight nod
Before the hammer falls
The call is prompt
A sale at trade
See the ripple of the water
At the next bridge
Roll against the tide
For as one suits
Playing games, a ball that shoots
A drowning sensation
Stopping short of a breath
Sold down the river
Up to your neck
Trust sometimes thrust upon thee
A life that's sold
The growth of the tree
Sold down the river
Let them be.

December 2013
4 Wednesday

MUSIC HAS THE STRENGTH

Messing Messiah
Hip hop to the wire
Rock and roll God
Devils in the fire
Shout to the masses
Release the cross
Where's the boss
Stoned out, thrown down
Blues to the soul
God's into rock and roll
Roll it up, rock it down
Indie town
Jesus has the jazz
Causing a slow-down commotion
Bring on the love for the music potion
Turn the tables, turn it round
Grounded to the sound
Bring it on, the power, the glory
Rap to the story
Music has the strength.

2013 December
Thursday 5

CHANGING

Changing stations
Changing lanes
Changing the strain
Changing round, begin again
Changing lights
Changing speed
Changing money, not into greed
Changing to the life you want
Changing of a religion, the heads in the font
Changing days to suit one's needs
Changing the world, mouths to feed
Changing the course
Changing the curse
Changing the saddle on the horse
Changing particles
Changing solidarity, I'm Spartacus
Changing the mind and soul, catharsis
Changing everything you want to change
Changing the rap, re-arrange to the change
Changing love for everyone
Changing rights
Changing life.

December 2013
6 Friday

E I T O P I T O S!

Contentment is reached
Who is the teacher?
A decision one makes to find the truth
A stolen heart will beat for somebody else
Disassociated with movement
Getting used to standing alone
Interrogating monotony
Something is foreseen
Start to begin to imagine
Freedom is on the other side of the coin
Both tails between two legs
Heads up on fantasy island
The right time is a myth
Too many obstacles to change the cause
The point is just to live
Create an illusion
A face with a different front
Clouding judgement for the onlooker
Everyone is their own protagonist in their own
story!

2013 December
Saturday 7

THE BARD OF YARDLEY

The bard of Yardley
Hardly a day goes by
Wake up, smell the air
Which way will the crow fly?
Days are more numbers
Numbers that are crunched
Taken from a count
Many, many days
That's a fair amount
The bard of Yardley
He writes a fair account.

Sunday 8

JUST BE

Just be you
Just be me
Just be yourself
Just be free
Just be happy
Just be, just be
Living.

December 2013
9 Monday

THIS IS MY CODE

A certain style
Its own uniqueness
Zen like matters I address
A message, hopefully of power
The power of freedom for everyone
Listen and take note
Tick or don't tick the box to vote
Follow the sheep through the gate
No, being oneself is how I demonstrate
Take, I shall not take
Give, I give everything
Writing down the words
The power and the page
From the pen, I release
All my rants and rage
To give the good their strength
Which I would go to great lengths
This is my way
This is my mode
This is me
This is my code.

2013 December
Tuesday 10

THERE'S NO RIGHT TIME

Movement inside the mind
A sweeping movement from the clock
Telling stories for a book
Stand clear, introduce the shock
Wake or be woken
Is a force of nature contrived?
Making love to a lover
There's no right time.

December 2013
11 Wednesday

MEMORIES ARE ALWAYS IN FASHION

Memories, washed up before our eyes
Soaking the pupil
Clouding the view
A thoughtful picture of a time gone by
Good, bad and distant
In a blink of an eye
Feeling secure within a time that has passed
A raised smile, this is my autograph
From the time we are born
There is a memory
The day before, our history
Collected remembrance
Many forgotten, a few, we save them
Memories are always in fashion.

DO I SEE A FUTURE?

Do I see a future?
Yes, I have seen the past
Present in the present
How long will it last?
It all lasts a lifetime
If you don't get, don't ask
You won't see it, never
The future hides behind it's mask
I don't see a future
This is what I meant
Do I see a future?
Only if it's Heaven sent.

December 2013
13 Friday

HAS SANTA EVER TRIED CRACK?

It's snowing up people's noses
It's going, the white stuff
What the f—k are they doing?
A-------s on trash
Weed, crack and hash
Smoking dope
F-----g dopes
Oh, they're cool
F-----g fools
Oh, look at me
Don't I look good
Act like everyone else
I think I should
W-----s on tap
Nose full of crap
Watch your family cry
If you die
Has Santa ever tried crack?
No chance, he would get the sack.

Saturday 14

THIS IS THE NIGHT

In the night, a cold chill
The vampires are out for blood
Necks are waiting to be drained
Teeth are sharpened
To the point of no return
Watch your back
The vampire bat
Hoping for daylight
This is the night.

Sunday 15

THIS IS THE DAY

In all your glory
Smiles create a story
It might not last
A day of amazement
Eyes are shining
A pleasure to say
This is the day.

December 2013
16 Monday

WHO'S THAT MESSING WITH YOUR MIND?

Who's that messing with your mind?
Who's that messing with your head?
Do me a favour
Close the door, don't let 'em in
Sister glycerine
Brother Dom
Father Lucifer
Pills and the Don
Uncle Judas
Auntie Sin
Shut that door
Don't let 'em in.

JUST A CASE OF FORTY WINKS

A mind field of dreams
Passing the time
Not awake, still asleep
Another world
A different zone
On the couch
Lazy at home
She lets me in to her pleasant world
A floating goddess
The most beautiful girl
Does she respond to my advances?
What are my chances?
Looking good to start
The part that drives you round the bend
Pisses you off when it comes to the end
It feels so real
At last I am with the woman of my dreams
So I think
It's just a case of forty winks.

December 2013
18 Wednesday

WITHIN POSSIBLE GRASP

Lingering moments
Worn out days
Judgement pushed upon thee
Build a note of trust
A wallowing wall of sound
The power of the healing sword
Cuts straight through the words
Rifles one's imagination into oblivion
Outshines any kind of emotion
Motionless fears
Realisation of those fears without moving
Inner sanctum
Cantankerous old concept of a fool
The ten second rule
Count to ten
Reach far and wide
To a place where all your dreams are
Within possible grasp.

2013 December
Thursday 19

THE CHRISTMAS CHILDREN

The Christmas children
In their beds
Waiting for Santa
On his sleigh
White and Red
Chimney soot
Snow is afoot
Christmas lights
Christmas children
Asleep at night
Carrots for the reindeers
Mince pies for Santa
A quick tot of brandy from the decanter
The tree looks magnificent
Festive, in all its glory
Christmas Eve
Like Mr Jones
Everything's Hunky Dory
Presents are left
Santa's work is done
Tomorrow the little ones become
The Christmas children.

December 2013
20 Friday

SCROOGE IS IN TOWN
PANTOMIME TIME

Ebenezer, counting his money
The old miser that is Scrooge
Face like a smacked arse
" A raise Bob Cratchit?"
"No, no, no, I refuse"
"I will see you tomorrow"
"Christmas Eve"
Bob mutters to himself
"I think his senses have taken leave"
The ghosts drop in to have a chat
Scrooge has a look of fear on his face
" Are you sure you have the right place?"
"We are here to tell you"
"Cratchit's family are skint"
"You should help them"
"Stop being an old skinflint"
"If you don't, we will kick your ass"
"Present, future, yes and I am Christmas past."

2013 December
Saturday 21

THE TURKEYS EAT THEIR CHRISTMAS LUNCH

Turkeys, Turkeys
They are a gobbling bunch
Out to eat their Christmas lunch
On their plates
Some of their best mates
No, that's us who eat their mates
The turkeys eat human meat
Off their china plates
Human meat, plenty of fat
Fair enough, tit for tat.

Sunday 22

DESTINY SPEAKS TO ME

Is anybody there?
I have heard it all before
Destiny speaks to me
Ah, show me the door then!

December 2013
23 Monday

I'M JUST ME

I'm just me at this time
Writing down this second line
Thinking of the third
But what about the fourth?
I have to reach the south of the page
The ink is still relatively north

I'm just me stuck in the middle
Not drawn to one or the other
I'm just me getting through this
I'm sure I will think of another

I'm just me at the bottom of the page
Trying to think of the end
I'm just me on my own
But do you know what?
I'm my best friend.

JC TO THE G

JC to the G
Write the rap to the page
Eminem is on the money
America's where he is made
JC to the G
I have never met them you see
Real or fake
That's the decision you make
JC is in the house
G is upstairs
One day you will take the stairway
Will they be there?
JC to the G
A nice idea
Are people frightened of the truth?
Inside, all that fear
JC to the G
The story is very old
It's not religion to me
A thought, I would like it to be true
You don't have to believe to see.

December 2013
25 Wednesday
Christmas Day Holiday

A CHRISTMAS THOUGHT

A way of hope
A ray of faith
Came into this world
A star was followed
Thou shall follow still.

2013 December
Thursday 26

A CHRISTMAS BOX

A mystery in a box
Takes centre stage
Is it empty?
Or a box that is full?
Footman or trade
A Christmas box.

December 2013
27 Friday

GO TO THE 28TH

A step in the right direction
Across to the other page
The diary is almost complete
The words, the lines
The message of peace written down
Effort and time, day by day
Five-minute rule to have my say
Pens with ink to clarify the day
Are things going great?
We will see
Go to the 28th.

2013 December
Saturday 28

GO TO THE 29TH

Writing more
Finding less
Less is more
More or less
Everything is easier
In hindsight
Go to the 29th.

Sunday 29

A WORN BOOK

A worn book
Battered exterior
Colour of grey
Words of the day
New Year, comes to pass
Beginning to the end
Comes at last
A kept book
Open it up, take a look
At the worn book.

December 2013
30 Monday

THE END OF THE BOOK IS NIGH

Many words
Feels like five
A year, a mixed bag
The penultimate poem
Another part of life goes on, fades out
Smiles on our faces as we shout
"Happy New Year"
To the next year we fly
The end of the book is nigh
"The last thing I wrote" will be the last thing I write
And in my book, it's not a lie
The end of the book is nigh
PS
"The last thing I wrote" was the last thing I wrote.

2013 December
Tuesday 31

THE FUTURE AND THE PAGE

Another year done
More hardship, not much fun
As cynical as a grumpy old man
That was not part of the plan
Change the course
Get rid of the curse
Things, could they get any worse?
I wrote this in the second month
Then I travelled into the future
And wrote this down
I could tear this page up
Go back and turn things round
Change the future and the page
R.I.P, THE PAGE
Until next year.

14391044R00185

Printed in Great Britain
by Amazon.co.uk, Ltd.,
Marston Gate.